MariaDB and MySQL Common Table Expressions and Window Functions Revealed

Daniel Bartholomew

Apress®

MariaDB and MySQL Common Table Expressions and Window Functions Revealed

Daniel Bartholomew
Raleigh, North Carolina, USA

ISBN-13 (pbk): 978-1-4842-3119-7 ISBN-13 (electronic): 978-1-4842-3120-3
https://doi.org/10.1007/978-1-4842-3120-3

Library of Congress Control Number: 2017958968

Managing Director: Welmoed Spahr
Editorial Director: Todd Green
Acquisitions Editor: Jonathan Gennick
Development Editor: Laura Berendson
Technical Reviewer: Stefan Ardeleanu
Coordinating Editor: Jill Balzano
Copy Editor: April Rondeau
Compositor: SPi Global
Indexer: SPi Global
Artist: SPi Global

Distributed to the book trade worldwide by Springer Science+Business Media New York, 233 Spring Street, 6th Floor, New York, NY 10013. Phone 1-800-SPRINGER, fax (201) 348-4505, email orders-ny@springer-sbm.com, or visit www.springeronline.com. Apress Media, LLC is a California LLC and the sole member (owner) is Springer Science + Business Media Finance Inc (SSBM Finance Inc). SSBM Finance Inc is a **Delaware** corporation.

For information on translations, please email rights@apress.com, or visit http://www.apress.com/rights-permissions.

Apress titles may be purchased in bulk for academic, corporate, or promotional use. eBook versions and licenses are also available for most titles. For more information, reference our Print and eBook Bulk Sales web page at http://www.apress.com/bulk-sales.

Any source code or other supplementary material referenced by the author in this book is available to readers on GitHub via the book's product page, located at www.apress.com/9781484231197. For more detailed information, please visit http://www.apress.com/source-code.

Printed on acid-free paper

For Amy, Ila, Lizzy, Anthon & Rachel.
I'm available to play more board games now, I promise.

Contents at a Glance

Contents

About the Author

Daniel Bartholomew has been using Linux since 1997 and databases since 1998. In addition to this book, he has written *MariaDB Cookbook* and *Getting Started with MariaDB* (1st and 2nd editions), as well as dozens of articles for various magazines, including *The Linux Journal*, *Linux Pro*, *Ubuntu User*, and *Tux*. Daniel became involved with the MariaDB project shortly after it began in early 2009 and continues to be involved to this day. He currently works for MariaDB, Inc., where he splits his time between managing MariaDB releases, writing new documentation, and maintaining the various bits and pieces that keep the MariaDB project running smoothly. Daniel is currently the official release manager for the MariaDB database.

About the Technical Reviewer

Stefan Ardeleanu was born in Bucharest, Romania, in 1967. He graduated with degrees in math and philosophy, and he was a math teacher for ten years. Afterward, he started a career in software development. He felt attracted to databases from the beginning, so his entire career in the software industry is related to databases—especially database development and design.

Stefan is a database specialist, a database architect, and a developer, and he has been working for many years under various systems, such as Oracle, SQL Server, DB2, and PostgreSQL. He has experience in OLTP and data warehouse and replication systems.

Stefan is a passionate SQL guy, and he was able to develop and improve a specific style of development. This style is reflected in his various projects, including replication systems and data-migration systems, where this style is highly required.

Stefan is also a database trainer, and he delivered courses in Oracle Chain as a partner, including database development courses and BI courses.

Acknowledgments

I'd like to thank Sergey Petrunia, Vicenţiu Ciorbaru, and others at MariaDB who were very helpful with the examples in this book. I'd also like to thank Jonathan Gennick, Jill Balzano, and the rest of the awesome people at Apress for shepherding this book from concept to completion.

Lastly, I'd like to thank Monty, Rasmus, and the many developers and users of MariaDB and MySQL. Working together, we've created something wonderful.

Introduction

In the software world, there are standards and implementations of those standards. Sometimes, the implementations come first, features introduced by eager developers trying to advance the state of the art, and they are formally standardized later. Other times, the standard comes first, developed and agreed upon by vendors, developers, and others, and then implementations of the standard—some faithful, others not so much—make their way into production software later on.

Common Table Expressions (CTEs) and Window Functions have been in the ANSI SQL standard for a long time. CTEs were introduced way back in the SQL99 version of the standard, and Window Functions were introduced in the SQL2003 version. Other database systems were quick(er) to implement both of them. Oracle, SQL Server, PostgreSQL, and even SQLite have had implementations of these features for years.

MariaDB and MySQL were somewhat late to the game, but they now have standards-compliant implementations of Window Functions and Common Table Expressions. MariaDB added them with their MariaDB 10.2 release, which was declared stable (GA) in May 2017. MySQL is introducing them as part of its upcoming 8.0 release, which as I write this is in its Release Candidate phase. The implementations were developed independently of each other, but they both stick close to the standard, so compatibility between them is good. Generally speaking, a query that works in MariaDB will most likely work in MySQL and vice versa. There are some differences, however, which this book notes when they come up.

Syntax

The syntax definitions in this book use the following conventions:

< > — Angle brackets surround elements, the name of which you provide. The brackets themselves are not part of the syntax and should not be included.

[ ] — Square brackets surround optional elements. They may be included, or not, depending on your choice. The brackets themselves are not part of the syntax and should not be included.

| — The pipe, or vertical bar, character separates groups of elements. You choose which of the elements you want to include in your statement. The pipe itself is not part of the syntax and should not be included.

... — An ellipsis, or three periods in a row, indicates that the prior section can be repeated. The ellipsis itself is not part of the syntax and should not be included.

( ) — Parentheses, where they appear, are part of the syntax and generally *must* be included in your SQL statement.

Words written in **UPPER CASE** are key words. They may be written in either *UPPER* or *lower* case, but must be written as shown. They also should not, and in some cases cannot, be generally used as the names of tables, functions, and other elements that you name.

Words written in **lower case** represent values that you provide. They may be integers, statements, or other elements of a SQL statement, as appropriate for the SQL statement being written.

PART I

■ ■ ■

Common Table Expressions

CHAPTER 1

■ ■ ■

Basics of Common Table Expressions

Common Table Expressions (CTEs) are one of the new SQL features introduced in MariaDB 10.2 and MySQL 8.0. This chapter will introduce CTEs, describe the two types, and explain the basic syntax. CTEs are named temporary result sets that only last for the duration of the query they are in. In some respects, they are similar to derived tables, but they are more powerful. They can refer to themselves recursively and can be referenced multiple times in the same query. They also enable column grouping and can be used as an alternative to views without our needing the `CREATE VIEW` permission. CTEs were first introduced as part of the SQL99 standard.

Before We Begin

Before we get into more detail on what CTEs are and what they can do, the examples in this chapter utilize sample data you can use to follow along with the text and experiment with CTEs yourself. The table used in this chapter is called employees and it can be created with the following query:

```
CREATE TABLE employees (
  id serial primary key,
  name VARCHAR(150) NOT NULL,
  title VARCHAR(100),
  office VARCHAR(100)
);
```

The data itself is in a CSV file called `bartholomew-ch01.csv`. It can be loaded with a query similar to the following (assuming the file is on the computer running MariaDB or MySQL server in the `/tmp/` folder):

```
LOAD DATA INFILE '/tmp/bartholomew-ch01.csv'
  INTO TABLE employees
  FIELDS TERMINATED BY ','
  OPTIONALLY ENCLOSED BY '"';
```

© Daniel Bartholomew 2017
D. Bartholomew, *MariaDB and MySQL Common Table Expressions and Window Functions Revealed*, https://doi.org/10.1007/978-1-4842-3120-3_1

If you are using MySQL 8.0, then the secure_file_priv setting is on by default. In this case, you will either need to move the file to the location specified in your config or turn off the setting in your my.cnf or my.ini file.

On Linux, the default location for secure_file_priv is /var/lib/mysql-files/, and on Windows it is C:\ProgramData\MySQL\MySQLServer 8.0\Uploads\; you'll need to move the files to that location before running the LOAD DATA command and then modify the command to point at that location instead of at the /tmp/ folder.

You can find out what your local MySQL installation's secure_file_priv setting is with the following command:

```
SHOW VARIABLES LIKE 'secure_file_priv';
```

We're now ready to begin.

■ **Tip**   When using the MySQL command-line client on Windows, you can use Linux-style paths with the LOAD DATA command. It's also worth mentioning that if you instead choose to use Windows-style paths, you will need to use double backslashes (\\) because the backslash character is used to escape other characters. For example, the following are equivalent:

```
LOAD DATA INFILE '/ProgramData/MySQL/MySQL Server 8.0/Uploads/file.csv'

LOAD DATA INFILE 'C:\\ProgramData\\MySQL\\MySQL Server 8.0\\Uploads\\file.csv'
```

What Are Common Table Expressions?

Common Table Expressions are commonly referred to as CTEs. Think of them as the result of a query that has a name you can refer to later on in your query. If a *named result set* sounds a little like a view or a derived table, that's because it is, but with some significant differences. We'll get to those in a second. First, what does a CTE look like?

Basic CTE Syntax

The general syntax for a Common Table Expression is as follows:

```
WITH <cte_name> AS (
  <cte_body>
)
<cte_query>
```

The WITH and AS keywords are what distinguish a CTE from a normal query. If you see a query that begins with WITH ... AS then you are looking at a CTE. The parts in angle brackets <> are what you provide. Let's go over the different parts now:

- **<cte_name>** is the name we will use to refer to the CTE later in our query; it can be any valid name, i.e., not a reserved word or function name.

- **<cte_body>** is just a SELECT statement that produces a result. This part is wrapped in parentheses ().

- **<cte_query>** is where we reference the <cte_name> in a SQL query. For example:

    SELECT <select_criteria> FROM <cte_name> [WHERE ...]

- **<select _criteria>** is your normal SELECT query criteria with optional WHERE and other clauses.

This might be a little difficult to visualize, so here's a basic valid CTE where we define a single *<cte_name>* and then SELECT from it. This CTE uses the sample data we loaded at the beginning of the chapter, so feel free to run it on your MariaDB or MySQL server.

```
WITH emp_raleigh AS (
  SELECT * FROM employees
    WHERE office='Raleigh'
)
SELECT * FROM emp_raleigh
  WHERE title != 'salesperson'
  ORDER BY title;
```

Let's break down what is happening here. Our *<cte_name>* is emp_raleigh, and it is a simple SELECT statement that selects every row in the employees table WHERE the office is Raleigh. You can think of this CTE as a view or filter of the employees table. Then, in the *<cte_query>* section, we use the *<cte_name>* as part of a simple query that looks for every entry where the employee is not a salesperson, and lastly it orders the results by their job title. Because the *<cte_query>* uses our emp_raleigh *<cte_name>*, our results will only come from records in the employees table WHERE office='Raleigh'.

Using our sample data, the result is:

```
+-----+-----------------+------------+---------+
| id  | name            | title      | office  |
+-----+-----------------+------------+---------+
|  73 | Mark Hamilton   | dba        | Raleigh |
|  77 | Nancy Porter    | dba        | Raleigh |
| 135 | Pauline Neal    | dba        | Raleigh |
|  68 | Edmund Hines    | manager    | Raleigh |
|  28 | Marc Greene     | programmer | Raleigh |
|  96 | Mary Walker     | programmer | Raleigh |
| 100 | Freida Duchesne | programmer | Raleigh |
+-----+-----------------+------------+---------+
```

So, apart from any salespeople there might be, our Raleigh office looks to be quite technical, just DBAs and programmers, apart from a single manager.

The Motivation for CTEs

The result from our simple example looks a lot like something you might use a derived table (AKA an inline view) or a view to get, both of which have existed in MariaDB and MySQL for years. Why would anyone ever want to use CTEs instead of the more familiar views or derived tables? Here are some reasons.

Temporary

First off, CTEs are temporary. A CTE is defined and used in the same query. A view, on the other hand, is more permanent and can be thought of as a somewhat permanent virtual table. This temporary nature of CTEs can be a good thing. Because the CTE and the query that uses it are all defined together, modifying it to keep up with updated business requirements is easy. Contrast that with a view, which needs to be updated separately from the queries that use it.

This temporary nature is part of the reason why derived tables are so popular; they let you quickly generate a useful temporary result set that you can perform operations on. CTEs build upon that usefulness with a more powerful set of features.

Readable

One big reason to use CTEs is because they are often more readable. Complex views or nested derived table queries can be hard for mere mortals to parse, often requiring reading the query inside-out, back-to-front, or some other unnatural order. Contrast that with CTEs, which generally can be read from top to bottom.

For example, here's our simple CTE example rewritten as a derived table:

```
SELECT * FROM (
  SELECT * FROM employees
    WHERE office='Raleigh'
) AS emp_raleigh
WHERE title != 'salesperson'
  ORDER BY title;
```

And so you don't have to go back and find it, here is the CTE version again:

```
WITH emp_raleigh AS (
  SELECT * FROM employees
    WHERE office='Raleigh'
)
SELECT * FROM emp_raleigh
  WHERE title != 'salesperson'
  ORDER BY title;
```

Unsurprisingly, the output of both queries, using our sample data, is the same. However, when you compare them, the CTE can be understood by simply reading it from beginning to end. To understand the derived table, on the other hand, you need to first read the inner SELECT statement and then jump up to the outer SELECT statement, and then back down to the end. On a simple example like this, the extra difficulty compared to the CTE is minimal, but as a derived table query becomes more complex, the difficulty in reading it goes up exponentially. For a CTE, however, the difficulty goes up in a more linear fashion because you can always just read from beginning to end, naturally.

Using in One or Many Places

Following on from the previous section, another reason to use CTEs is if you need something complex for just one query as opposed to something that will be used many times in many different queries. For example, if your underlying sales table stores invoice dates using a Unix timestamp, but several of your applications expect YYYY-MM-DD whenever they query the table, a view would be an excellent solution; just define the view and have your applications call that. On the other hand, a complex view only used once in a single application might be more maintainable if rewritten as an easier-to-read CTE.

Permissions

When working on your own personal databases on your own workstation or server, your database user generally has the ALL PRIVILEGES WITH GRANT OPTION permissions, which means you can do anything you need or want to your tables and databases, including CREATE, UPDATE, INSERT, DELETE, and so on. Or, you might regularly just log in as the *root* database user, which automatically has all permissions. Databases used in production, however, generally have more granular access defined. Some users are only able to SELECT from tables in certain databases, while others can make inserts in some tables but not in others, and yet other users are given more or fewer grants depending on their various job functions.

You may find yourself in need of something like a view on a table that you do not have the CREATE VIEW permission on. CTEs only require the SELECT permission, so in this case using a CTE is a great way to get what you need without having to pester one of the DBAs to either create the view you need for you or asking them to grant you the CREATE VIEW permission on the table you need it on, which they may be unable to do because of company policies.

Nesting

CTEs bring several new tricks to our DBA toolbox, one of which is that in each individual <cte_body> we can refer to other CTEs. This solves a big problem with nested derived tables where every level of nesting greatly increases the complexity.

For example, let's expand upon our simple CTE example and drill further into our data by defining a second *<cte_name>* with its accompanying *<cte_body>* that selects just the DBAs in the Raleigh office:

```
WITH emp_raleigh AS (
  SELECT * FROM employees
    WHERE office='Raleigh'
),
emp_raleigh_dbas AS (
  SELECT * from emp_raleigh
    WHERE title='dba'
)
SELECT * FROM emp_raleigh_dbas;
```

Looking at this code, we have our original *<cte_name>*, emp_raleigh, and its *<cte_body>*. We then define a second *<cte_name>*, emp_raleigh_dbas, and its *<cte_body>*. emp_raleigh_dbas builds upon emp_raleigh by only looking for records WHERE title='dba'. Lastly, in the *<cte_query>* section we SELECT everything from emp_raleigh_dbas. Syntactically, this is much more readable than the equivalent query written using a nested derived table.

Using our sample data, the result is as follows:

```
+-----+---------------+-------+---------+
| id  | name          | title | office  |
+-----+---------------+-------+---------+
|  73 | Mark Hamilton | dba   | Raleigh |
|  77 | Nancy Porter  | dba   | Raleigh |
| 135 | Pauline Neal  | dba   | Raleigh |
+-----+---------------+-------+---------+
```

Multiplexing

Building upon the ability to define multiple *<cte_name>*s in the same query with their corresponding *<cte_body>*s, we have the ability to refer to a given *<cte_name>* multiple times, either in a following *<cte_body>* section or in the *<cte_query>* section. As an example of referring to a single *<cte_name>* multiple times, here is an anti-self-join that looks for DBAs that are the only DBA at their particular office:

```
WITH dbas AS (
  SELECT * FROM employees
    WHERE title='dba'
)
SELECT * FROM dbas A1
  WHERE NOT EXISTS (
    SELECT 1 FROM dbas A2
      WHERE
        A2.office=A1.office
      AND
        A2.name <> A1.name
  );
```

Here, our dbas *<cte_name>* simply selects all of the DBAs in the company, then in our ending *<cte_query>* we refer to dbas two times in order to filter out all DBAs except those we are interested in.

Using our sample data, the result is as follows:

```
+----+---------------+-------+---------+
| id | name          | title | office  |
+----+---------------+-------+---------+
|  6 | Toby Lucas    | dba   | Wichita |
| 16 | Susan Charles | dba   | Nauvoo  |
+----+---------------+-------+---------+
```

I think management should make sure Toby and Susan visit other offices in the company a few times every year, just so they don't feel isolated from the other DBAs in the company.

Recursion

The last reason why CTEs are so useful is that they can be recursive. Within their own *<cte_body>* they can call themselves. This technique provides a lot of power. But let's not get ahead of ourselves—there's a whole chapter devoted to these types of CTE queries, so we won't talk about it more here.

Summary

In this chapter, we covered the basic syntax of CTEs as well as some of the reasons why this feature was added to the SQL standard and is now being added to MariaDB and MySQL. We also went through a couple of simple examples of non-recursive CTEs.

We'll dive deeper into non-recursive CTEs in the next chapter, then look at recursive CTEs in Chapter 3.

CHAPTER 2

■ ■ ■

Non-recursive Common Table Expressions

You already got a taste of non-recursive CTEs in the previous chapter. This chapter will expand upon the previous examples and show more of the things you can do with non-recursive CTEs. In this chapter, we'll cover some common uses of CTEs and finish with how to convert existing queries that use subqueries into queries that use CTEs.

Before We Begin

As with the previous chapter, the examples in this chapter utilize sample data. In addition to the employees table we used previously, in this chapter we'll use a table called commissions. This table can be created with the following query:

```
CREATE TABLE commissions (
  id serial primary key,
  salesperson_id BIGINT(20) NOT NULL,
  commission_id BIGINT(20) NOT NULL,
  commission_amount DECIMAL(12,2) NOT NULL,
  commission_date DATE NOT NULL
);
```

The data is in a CSV file called bartholomew-ch02.csv. It can be loaded with a query similar to the following (assuming the file is on the computer running MariaDB or MySQL server in the /tmp/ folder):

```
LOAD DATA INFILE '/tmp/bartholomew-ch02.csv'
  INTO TABLE commissions
  FIELDS TERMINATED BY ','
  OPTIONALLY ENCLOSED BY '"';
```

© Daniel Bartholomew 2017
D. Bartholomew, *MariaDB and MySQL Common Table Expressions and Window Functions Revealed*, https://doi.org/10.1007/978-1-4842-3120-3_2

■ **Note**   See the "Before We Begin" section of Chapter 1 for extra information about loading the files on Windows and working around issues with `secure_file_priv`.

We're now ready to begin.

Using CTEs for Year-over-Year Comparisons

In the previous chapter, we introduced the ability to refer to a CTE multiple times in a single query. Let's explore a more substantial example.

One thing many companies like to track is how sales improve (or not) year-over-year. In our sample `commissions` table, we track the commissions each of the company's 55 salespersons have earned and when they earned them. One day, the CEO comes to us and says that he wants to compare how the salespersons are doing from one year to the next. A fairly straightforward traditional SQL query can easily get us the data we want, grouped by salesperson and year:

```
SELECT
  salesperson_id,
  YEAR(commission_date) AS year,
  SUM(commission_amount) AS total
FROM
  commissions
GROUP BY
  salesperson_id, year;
```

Our sample data contains commissions data for the years 2016 and 2017, so this query gives us 110 rows—two rows for each of our 55 salespersons. Here's the truncated result:

```
+----------------+------+----------+
| salesperson_id | year | total    |
+----------------+------+----------+
|              3 | 2016 | 2249.93  |
|              3 | 2017 | 3449.67  |
|              7 | 2016 | 1088.32  |
|              7 | 2017 | 3197.25  |
|              8 | 2016 | 4514.73  |
|              8 | 2017 | 5178.19  |
|             10 | 2016 | 9433.58  |
|             10 | 2017 | 8479.05  |
...
+----------------+------+----------+
```

We could call this complete and send the data to the CEO, but by using a CTE we can do much better.

Using our initial query as our *<cte_body>*, we can select from the data twice, using a
WHERE clause to set up the condition to select a given year and the previous year together.
Here's what it could look like:

```
WITH commissions_year AS (
  SELECT
    salesperson_id,
    YEAR(commission_date) AS year,
    SUM(commission_amount) AS total
  FROM
    commissions
  GROUP BY
    salesperson_id, year
)
SELECT *
FROM
  commissions_year CUR,
  commissions_year PREV
WHERE
  CUR.salesperson_id=PREV.salesperson_id AND
  CUR.year=PREV.year + 1;
```

After setting up the CTE, which we called commissions_year, we selected from
it twice—once as CUR and once as PREV. The WHERE clause is where we match the
salesperson_id fields from both and set up the condition that we're comparing a year
with another year that is one more (+1) from it.

This time, the output looks like the following:

```
+----------------+------+----------+----------------+------+----------+
| salesperson_id | year | total    | salesperson_id | year | total    |
+----------------+------+----------+----------------+------+----------+
|              3 | 2017 | 3449.67  |              3 | 2016 | 2249.93  |
|              7 | 2017 | 3197.25  |              7 | 2016 | 1088.32  |
|              8 | 2017 | 5178.19  |              8 | 2016 | 4514.73  |
|             10 | 2017 | 8479.05  |             10 | 2016 | 9433.58  |
...
+----------------+------+----------+----------------+------+----------+
```

This presentation is better, but we could do without the duplicated salesperson_id
columns, and while we're at it, we should JOIN with the employees table to get the
employee name in the output (something our CEO would appreciate).

We'll add the JOIN to the FROM clause in our *<cte_body>*, then we'll select just
the columns we want from the *<cte_query>* section to be in the output. With those
modifications, our complete CTE now looks like this:

```
WITH commissions_year AS (
  SELECT
    employees.id AS sp_id,
```

```
    employees.name AS salesperson,
    YEAR(commission_date) AS year,
    SUM(commission_amount) AS total
  FROM
    commissions LEFT JOIN employees
      ON commissions.salesperson_id = employees.id
  GROUP BY
    sp_id, year
)
SELECT CUR.sp_id, CUR.salesperson, PREV.year, PREV.total, CUR.year, CUR.
total
FROM
  commissions_year CUR,
  commissions_year PREV
WHERE
  CUR.sp_id=PREV.sp_id AND
  CUR.year=PREV.year + 1;
```

And our output now looks like the following:

```
+-------+--------------------+------+----------+------+----------+
| sp_id | salesperson        | year | total    | year | total    |
+-------+--------------------+------+----------+------+----------+
|     3 | Evelyn Alexander   | 2016 | 2249.93  | 2017 | 3449.67  |
|     7 | John Conner        | 2016 | 1088.32  | 2017 | 3197.25  |
|     8 | Leo Gutierrez      | 2016 | 4514.73  | 2017 | 5178.19  |
|    10 | Ryan Fletcher      | 2016 | 9433.58  | 2017 | 8479.05  |
...
+-------+--------------------+------+----------+------+----------+
```

Now it is very easy for the CEO to see at a glance that while Evelyn, John, and Leo increased their commissions from 2016 to 2017, Ryan's commissions are down by around $1,000 from 2016 to 2017. Maybe he needs some coaching from his manager?

And if the CEO comes back and wants a filtered list showing just those salespersons whose sales went down from year to year, we can simply add the following to the end of our *<cte_query>* section:

```
AND CUR.total < PREV.total;
```

An equivalent analytical query using derived tables would be much larger and not nearly as readable and concise.

Comparing Individuals Against Their Group

One annoying issue with using subqueries is when you have to copy and paste them multiple times in your query. These duplicated FROM (SELECT ...) statements are prime locations for errors, especially when something changes and you need to update every single one of them. CTEs provide a way to eliminate this duplication. A given <cte_body> is defined once and tied to a single <cte_name>. Whenever you need it, you just reference the <cte_name>, and if something needs to be updated, you just have to update the <cte_body> in one place.

Using the same base CTE as from the previous example, we can modify the SELECT statement after it to easily perform a different kind of analytical query, one that traditionally would have used duplicated FROM (SELECT...) statements. This time, instead of comparing salespersons to their own performance from one year to the next, we'll compare them to all salespersons. In particular, in his next company-wide email, the CEO wants to give a shout-out to all of the salespersons who made at least 2 percent of the total commissions earned by all salespersons in the entire company during 2017.

```
WITH commissions_year AS (
  SELECT
    employees.id AS sp_id,
    employees.name AS salesperson,
    YEAR(commission_date) AS year,
    SUM(commission_amount) AS total
  FROM
    commissions LEFT JOIN employees
      ON commissions.salesperson_id = employees.id
  GROUP BY
    sp_id, year
)
SELECT *
FROM
  commissions_year C1
WHERE
  total > ( SELECT
              0.02*SUM(total)
            FROM
              commissions_year C2
            WHERE
              C2.year = C1.year
            AND C2.year = 2017)
ORDER BY
  total DESC;
```

The <cte_body> for commissions_year is unchanged from our previous example, so there's no need to go over it. The difference is all in the <cte_query> section. Our SELECT statement looks at individual totals that make up at least 2 percent of the total of all commissions for the 2017 year, then orders everything DESC so the top earner is on top.

Doing this sort of query in the traditional way would mean each FROM in the <cte_query> section would be a copy-pasted FROM (SELECT...) statement.

If you've been following along with the examples, the output of the preceding code looks like the following:

```
+-------+-------------------+------+----------+
| sp_id | salesperson       | year | total    |
+-------+-------------------+------+----------+
|   116 | Christian Reeves  | 2017 | 13856.74 |
|    69 | Luis Vaughn       | 2017 | 12570.95 |
|   128 | Stephanie Dawson  | 2017 | 12253.44 |
|    38 | Dorothy Anderson  | 2017 | 12010.91 |
|    78 | Louis Santiago    | 2017 | 11423.48 |
|   131 | Rene Gibbs        | 2017 | 11147.38 |
|   121 | Christina Terry   | 2017 | 10979.07 |
|    53 | Jennifer Moore    | 2017 | 10967.64 |
|   114 | Veronica Boone    | 2017 | 10651.10 |
|    41 | Terrance Reese    | 2017 | 10219.33 |
|   132 | Alan Carroll      | 2017 | 10066.97 |
|    34 | Bobby French      | 2017 | 9928.69  |
|   105 | Alonzo Page       | 2017 | 9782.69  |
|    66 | Kathryn Barnes    | 2017 | 9433.56  |
|   106 | Bradley Black     | 2017 | 9387.77  |
|   118 | Deborah Peterson  | 2017 | 9265.96  |
|    79 | Rafael Sandoval   | 2017 | 9055.54  |
+-------+-------------------+------+----------+
```

Let's give a round of applause to the members of the 2017 2 Percent Club!

Translating Subqueries into CTEs

Let's switch gears and talk about the process for taking an existing query and translating it into a CTE. It is fairly simple. To illustrate this, here's a query that is equivalent to our query from the previous example, but instead of using a CTE, it uses subqueries in the form of two identical FROM (SELECT...) statements:

```
SELECT *
FROM (
  SELECT
    employees.id AS sp_id,
    employees.name AS salesperson,
    YEAR(commission_date) AS year,
    SUM(commission_amount) AS total
  FROM
    commissions LEFT JOIN employees
      ON commissions.salesperson_id = employees.id
```

```
GROUP BY
    sp_id, year
    ) AS C1
WHERE
    total > ( SELECT
                0.02*SUM(total)
             FROM (
               SELECT
                 employees.id AS sp_id,
                 employees.name AS salesperson,
                 YEAR(commission_date) AS year,
                 SUM(commission_amount) AS total
               FROM
                 commissions LEFT JOIN employees
                   ON commissions.salesperson_id = employees.id
               GROUP BY
                 sp_id, year
               ) AS C2
             WHERE
             C2.year = C1.year
             AND C2.year = 2017)
ORDER BY
    total DESC;
```

Because of the duplicated FROM (SELECT...) statements, this query is 33 lines long, as opposed to the 25-line CTE that does the same thing. An eight-line difference isn't much, but more-complex queries could include five, seven, eleven, or even more duplicated subqueries, causing an almost exponential increase in the size of the query. This could quickly turn into a maintenance nightmare if something in the underlying table(s) changes and we need to update the query.

To convert a query with duplicated subqueries into a CTE, there are only three steps (four if you need to repeat the process for additional duplicated subqueries):

1. Locate the first occurrence of the derived table query and copy it above the SELECT line, wrapping it in WITH <cte_name> AS (and then an ending).

2. Replace that first occurrence of the subquery with whatever we put as the <cte_name>.

3. Go through the rest of the query and find the additional identical subqueries and replace them with <cte_name> as well.

4. (Optional) Repeat the process for any other duplicated subqueries in your query, if any.

Not every query will be a perfect fit for this process, but many queries are.

Summary

In this chapter, we expanded upon the examples from the previous chapter and went through a couple more-substantial examples that illustrated how CTEs are superior to subqueries, particularly in how they help us avoid duplicated subqueries that are hard to modify and maintain. We then finished with a discussion of how to take a query that uses subqueries and convert it into a query that uses CTEs instead.

To round out the CTE section of this book, the next chapter will cover what I think is the most exciting part of CTEs—recursion.

CHAPTER 3

■ ■ ■

Recursive Common Table Expressions

Recursion is a very useful technique in computer science. Recursive algorithms are well suited for navigating data structures such as *trees*, where items contain other items that may also contain items, and *graphs*, which track connections or routes between items. SQL has historically done a poor job with these.

Oracle attempted to add recursive support to SQL in the 1980s with their non-standard CONNECT BY syntax, but this has now been superseded, improved upon, and standardized in the official SQL standard, version SQL99, with recursive CTEs. Implementations of this standard started appearing in various databases, such as Oracle and SQL Server, starting around 2007, with MariaDB and MySQL finally catching up and getting them about ten years after that.

In simple terms, a recursive CTE is a CTE that refers to itself in its *<cte_body>*. Having a CTE refer to itself might seem complicated, but once you get the hang of it, it isn't bad, and by using recursion there are a lot of cool things you can do. This chapter will provide examples showing some of the things you can do with recursive CTEs.

Before We Begin

As with the other chapters, the examples in this chapter utilize sample data. For this chapter, we'll be using two tables, one called tudors and another called routes. The tudors table can be created with the following query:

```
CREATE TABLE tudors (
  id serial primary key,
  name VARCHAR(100) NOT NULL,
  father BIGINT(20),
  mother BIGINT(20)
);
```

D. Bartholomew, *MariaDB and MySQL Common Table Expressions and Window Functions Revealed*, https://doi.org/10.1007/978-1-4842-3120-3_3

The data is in a CSV file called `bartholomew-ch03-tudors.csv`. It can be loaded with a query similar to the following (assuming the file is on the computer running MariaDB or MySQL server in the /tmp/ folder):

```
LOAD DATA INFILE '/tmp/bartholomew-ch03-tudors.csv'
  INTO TABLE tudors
  FIELDS TERMINATED BY ','
  OPTIONALLY ENCLOSED BY '"';
```

The routes table can be created with the following query:

```
CREATE TABLE routes (
  id serial primary key,
  departing VARCHAR(100) NOT NULL,
  arriving VARCHAR(100) NOT NULL
);
```

The data is in a CSV file called `bartholomew-ch03-routes.csv`. It can be loaded with a query similar to the following (assuming the file is on the computer running MariaDB or MySQL server in the /tmp/ folder):

```
LOAD DATA INFILE '/tmp/bartholomew-ch03-routes.csv'
  INTO TABLE routes
  FIELDS TERMINATED BY ','
  OPTIONALLY ENCLOSED BY '"';
```

■ **Note**   See the "Before We Begin" section of Chapter 1 for extra information about loading the files on Windows and working around issues with `secure_file_priv`.

We're now ready to begin.

Recursive CTE Syntax

The syntax for recursive CTE queries is similar to that for non-recursive CTEs, with a couple differences. Here's the basic syntax:

```
WITH RECURSIVE <cte_name> AS (
  <anchor>
  UNION [ALL]
  <recursive>
)
<cte_query>
```

Right away, you'll notice the introduction of the RECURSIVE keyword. This must be included for recursive CTEs in MariaDB and MySQL. This keyword is not required for recursive CTEs in other databases, such as Oracle and SQL Server.

The other difference from non-recursive CTEs is that the *<cte_body>* is split into two parts, with a UNION or UNION ALL separating the two. The first part is the *<anchor>*. It is a non-recursive query similar to the *<cte_body>* of a non-recursive CTE. Then, after the UNION or UNION ALL, there is the recursive part. This part will contain references to the *<cte_name>*, which is what makes the CTE recursive, so we'll call this part *<recursive>* for simplicity.

Adding Numbers

The biggest thing to keep in mind when getting started with recursive CTEs is that the way recursion actually works might not be exactly how we would expect it to work.

We can illustrate this by working through a good, if artificial, example of how recursive CTEs work: adding numbers together. Suppose we want to add all of the numbers from 1 through 100 together. Figuring it out by hand with $1 + 2 + 3 + 4 + \ldots + 100$ would be very tedious. It would be much better to have a recursive loop that does the repetitive parts for me. This example has the benefit of not requiring us to create any tables. Don't worry, we'll get to our tudors and routes tables later in the chapter.

To get us started adding our numbers together, we want a loop that does the following:

1. Takes the current number and adds it to the current total

2. Adds 1 to the current number

3. Repeats until the current number equals 100

To start things out, we'll want to have two columns—one for the counter keeping track of the current number and another for the total. We'll call these Count and Total, respectively, and we'll start from zero. The simplest way to express this in SQL is like so:

```
SELECT
  0 AS Count,
  0 AS Total
```

This will be our *<anchor>*, the point we start from.

Now, we need to add 1 to Count and add the current Count to the Total. This will be our *<recursive>* part. Here it is in SQL:

```
SELECT
  Count + 1,
  Total + Count
```

By adding a WITH RECURSIVE TotalSum AS part to the front, a UNION ALL between the two sample queries, a FROM to refer to our *<cte_name>*, a WHERE clause so we know when the CTE will finish, and lastly a simple SELECT * FROM <cte_name> as our output, we get a CTE query that looks like the following:

```
WITH RECURSIVE TotalSum AS (
  SELECT
    0 AS Count,
    0 AS Total
  UNION ALL
  SELECT
    Count + 1,
    Total + Count
  FROM TotalSum
  WHERE Count <= 100
)
SELECT * FROM TotalSum;
```

This looks reasonable, but when we run this query, things don't look exactly right:

Count	Total
0	0
1	0
2	1
3	3
4	6
5	10
...	
96	4560
97	4656
98	4753
99	4851
100	4950
101	5050

The Count column looks fine, until we get to the end when it stops at *101* instead of *100* like we wanted. Also, while the Total column ends up with the correct answer, *5050*, it's confusing because at the beginning when Count is *1*, Total is still equal to *0*, and at the end when Count is *101*, the total of *5050* is after adding the final *100*, not after adding *101*.

This behavior can be explained with an understanding of how the database is performing the UNION ALL between the *<anchor>* and *<recursive>* parts of our TotalSum CTE.

First, when we begin, Count and Total are both set to 0, and the first line of our output reflects that:

```
+-------+-------+
| Count | Total |
+-------+-------+
|     0 |     0 |
+-------+-------+
```

We then do a UNION ALL against this table with our Count + 1 and Total + Count expressions. Count + 1 = 0 + 1 = 1, but Total + Count = 0 + 0 = 0, because when the value of Count is calculated, the value of Count is being pulled from the previous output, not the expression one line above that adds 1 to Count. The UNION ALL is only looking at the previous row of output, and in that row, Count = 0. So, our second line of output may look wrong, but from the database's perspective, it is completely accurate:

```
+-------+-------+
| Count | Total |
+-------+-------+
|     1 |     0 |
+-------+-------+
```

The fix then, is pretty simple. When calculating the Total column, we add one to it just like we do to the Count column. With this change, we should also change the WHERE Count <= 100 to WHERE Count < 100 because by the time Count actually reaches 100 we're already done. With those modifications, our recursive CTE now looks like the following:

```
WITH RECURSIVE TotalSum AS (
  SELECT
    0 AS Count,
    0 AS Total
  UNION ALL
  SELECT
    Count + 1,
    Total + Count + 1
  FROM TotalSum
  WHERE Count < 100
)
SELECT * FROM TotalSum;
```

The output of this version looks much better, exactly what we would expect:

```
+-------+-------+
| Count | Total |
+-------+-------+
|     0 |     0 |
|     1 |     1 |
|     2 |     3 |
|     3 |     6 |
|     4 |    10 |
|     5 |    15 |
...
|    96 |  4656 |
|    97 |  4753 |
|    98 |  4851 |
|    99 |  4950 |
|   100 |  5050 |
+-------+-------+
```

The key takeaway from this exercise is to remember that the *<recursive>* part after a UNION or UNION ALL is looking at the previously retrieved or calculated row, *not* the current row, when making its calculations.

Calculating Fibonacci Numbers

Another interesting application of recursion is to calculate the Fibonacci sequence. In this series of numbers, every new number in the sequence is calculated as the sum of the previous two. Because the sequence relies on two numbers, we must define two; we can choose either 0 and 1, or 1 and 1. For this example, we'll go with the former and call them Current and Next. A simple bit of SQL that does this for our *<anchor>* part is:

```
SELECT
  0 AS Current,
  1 AS Next
```

For our *<recursive>* part, our loop needs to do the following:

1. Move Current to Next.

2. Calculate the new Next by adding Current + Next.

3. Repeat until we say stop.

The math part is straightforward:

```
SELECT
  Next AS Current,
  Current + Next AS Next
```

Putting both together, with an upper limit set at 1000 and a simple SELECT * FROM <cte_name> as our output, we get the following:

```
WITH RECURSIVE fibonacci AS (
  SELECT
    0 AS Current,
    1 AS Next
  UNION ALL
  SELECT
    Next AS Current,
    Current + Next AS Next
  FROM fibonacci
  WHERE Next < 1000
)
SELECT * FROM fibonacci;
```

The output of this recursive CTE looks like this:

```
+---------+------+
| Current | Next |
+---------+------+
|       0 |    1 |
|       1 |    1 |
|       1 |    2 |
|       2 |    3 |
|       3 |    5 |
|       5 |    8 |
|       8 |   13 |
|      13 |   21 |
|      21 |   34 |
|      34 |   55 |
|      55 |   89 |
|      89 |  144 |
|     144 |  233 |
|     233 |  377 |
|     377 |  610 |
|     610 |  987 |
|     987 | 1597 |
+---------+------+
```

As with the previous example, this result is probably not exactly what we want. Instead of a simple Fibonacci sequence, we have parallel series, with the Current and Next columns off by one in sequence order. The reason for this, again, relates to how the *recursive* part is calculated.

When we start, Current = 0 and Next = 1. That is the first row in our output:

```
+---------+------+
| Current | Next |
+---------+------+
|       0 |    1 |
+---------+------+
```

In our first run through the *<recursive>* part, we first move the value of Next (1) to Current so that for the *following* row, Current will be equal to 1. We then set Next to Current + Next of the initial row, or 0 + 1, or *1*. So, for the second row, both Current and Next are equal to 1:

```
+---------+------+
| Current | Next |
+---------+------+
|       1 |    1 |
+---------+------+
```

The loop now repeats, and in the *<recursive>* part we move the value of Next from the second row to Current. So, for the third row it will still be *1*. Then, we set the value of Next to the second-row values of Current + Next, or 1 + 1, or *2*. So, for the third row the values are:

```
+---------+------+
| Current | Next |
+---------+------+
|       1 |    2 |
+---------+------+
```

This process repeats until our WHERE condition is met, which happens when the loop looks at the 17th row, with the side effect being that we get output beyond our *1000* limit because until that point the value of Next was always less than that.

To get the output we want—a single column containing a Fibonacci sequence where the highest number is less than 1000—you can probably guess what we have to do: we simply SELECT the Current column from our CTE instead of selecting all columns. We can rename it to further improve the output:

```
WITH RECURSIVE fibonacci AS (
  SELECT
    0 AS Current,
    1 AS Next
  UNION ALL
  SELECT
    Next AS Current,
    Current + Next AS Next
  FROM fibonacci
  WHERE Next < 1000
)
SELECT Current AS fibonacci_series FROM fibonacci;
```

Now, the output of our `fibonacci` CTE looks like this:

```
+------------------+
| fibonacci_series |
+------------------+
|                0 |
|                1 |
|                1 |
|                2 |
|                3 |
|                5 |
|                8 |
|               13 |
|               21 |
|               34 |
|               55 |
|               89 |
|              144 |
|              233 |
|              377 |
|              610 |
|              987 |
+------------------+
```

Some additional things we could do here include setting up a counter to track which position of the Fibonacci sequence we are at, and maybe using that as our limiter instead of the actual Fibonacci value we are at. For example, we could modify our CTE and calculate the Fibonacci sequence to 100 places.

Looking Up Ancestors in a Tree

Using recursive CTEs to solve math problems, as in the previous two examples, or even creating a recursive CTE Sieve of Eratosthenes, can be fun little diversions, but they aren't often practical in the real world. So, let's move away from those and tackle some examples that you might actually run into. We'll start with using the `tudors` table.

This table contains data on the Tudor monarchs of England— you know, Henry VIII, Elizabeth I, Bloody Mary, those guys. There are four columns: `id`, `name`, `father`, and `mother`. The `father` and `mother` columns, if populated, point to the records for the father and mother of the person in question, like you would expect.

The data starts with Elizabeth I and then contains several generations back, as well as some of her cousins, aunts, and uncles. Conveniently, her `id` is 1. Here's the SQL to pull up her record:

```
SELECT * FROM tudors
WHERE id = 1;
```

The result looks like this:

```
+----+-----------------------+--------+--------+
| id | name                  | father | mother |
+----+-----------------------+--------+--------+
|  1 | Elizabeth I of England |      2 |      3 |
+----+-----------------------+--------+--------+
```

To find her parents without using a CTE, there are many things we could do; for example, here is one way using a simple JOIN:

```
SELECT
  elizabeth.id, elizabeth.name, tudors.id, tudors.name
FROM
  tudors AS elizabeth
    JOIN tudors ON
        tudors.id = elizabeth.father
      OR
        tudors.id = elizabeth.mother
WHERE elizabeth.id=1;
```

This query isn't the easiest to read, but it's not too bad. The result looks like this:

```
+----+-----------------------+----+-----------------------+
| id | name                  | id | name                  |
+----+-----------------------+----+-----------------------+
|  1 | Elizabeth I of England |  2 | Henry VIII of England |
|  1 | Elizabeth I of England |  3 | Anne Boleyn           |
+----+-----------------------+----+-----------------------+
```

This result gives us Elizabeth's parents, but what if we want to pull up all of Elizabeth's ancestors: parents, grandparents, great-grandparents, and so on? This is the type of query that recursive CTEs were made for.

For the *<anchor>* part of our query, we can use the query that just retrieves Elizabeth's record, and for the *<recursive>* part, we can use something that resembles our JOIN-based query but makes more sense, syntactically:

```
WITH RECURSIVE elizabeth AS (
  SELECT * FROM tudors
  WHERE id = 1
UNION
  SELECT tudors.*
  FROM tudors, elizabeth
  WHERE
    tudors.id = elizabeth.father OR
    tudors.id = elizabeth.mother
)
SELECT * FROM elizabeth;
```

Using a *<cte_name>* of elizabeth both does and doesn't make sense. It makes sense because for the first run through the loop we actually are looking for Elizabeth's father and mother. It doesn't make sense for future runs of the loop, because on the second pass through the loop we are looking for the parents of Henry VIII and Anne Boleyn, Elizabeth's grandparents, and for the third loop her great-grandparents, and so on.

However, for me at least, the name helped when writing the *<recursive>* part. Thinking recursively is hard enough, so any advantage that can be found in naming CTEs is a good thing.

The (truncated) result of this query looks like this:

```
+----+--------------------------------------------+--------+--------+
| id | name                                       | father | mother |
+----+--------------------------------------------+--------+--------+
|  1 | Elizabeth I of England                     |      2 |      3 |
|  2 | Henry VIII of England                      |      4 |      5 |
|  3 | Anne Boleyn                                |      6 |      7 |
|  4 | Henry VII of England                       |      8 |      9 |
|  5 | Elizabeth of York                          |     10 |     11 |
|  6 | Thomas Boleyn, 1st Earl of Wiltshire       |     12 |     13 |
|  7 | Elizabeth Howard                           |     14 |     15 |
|  8 | Edmund Tudor, 1st Earl of Richmond         |     16 |     17 |
|  9 | Margaret Beaufort                          |     18 |     19 |
| 10 | Edward IV of England                       |     20 |     21 |
...
+----+--------------------------------------------+--------+--------+
```

You'll notice that for this recursive CTE there is a WHERE clause, like our previous ones, but it doesn't have a set stopping point like WHERE tudors.id < 100. So, how does the CTE know when it is done? To find out, let's walk through what the query is doing step by step.

First, there is our *<anchor>*, and during the first pass its result is output. Then, the *<recursive>* part looks for records where the father or mother fields match the id. Those that it finds are joined to the result table.

The CTE then loops back and does the same search again, this time incorporating the previous results in the UNION and ignoring records it finds that are already in the result table. This process repeats until no new results are returned. That is the trigger for the CTE to stop looping.

For our sample data, looping until nothing new is returned is no problem, as it only loops a handful of times. But what if we are navigating an enormous tree of data? What's to prevent our query from looping endlessly?

The answer depends on whether you are using MariaDB or MySQL.

In MariaDB, as a final safety measure, there is a @@max_recursive_iterations variable that governs the maximum number of loops the server will make before stopping. You can show its current value with:

```
SHOW VARIABLES LIKE '%recursive%';
```

The default setting is very high, 4294967295, which should be fine for almost all queries, but it can be changed, like any other variable, if needed. Setting it to 0 disables it, which should be done cautiously.

As of right now, there is no corresponding variable in MySQL. There, the only current protection is to set @@max_statement_time to the maximum amount of time you will allow a query to run until it should be killed.

Finding All Possible Destinations

Our last two examples in this chapter use the routes table. This table contains a list of hypothetical train routes between various cities in North America. Each route has a departing city and an arriving city. Between some cities there are two routes—one in each direction. In other cities, the route only goes in one direction. Figure 3-1 shows all of the routes and cities.

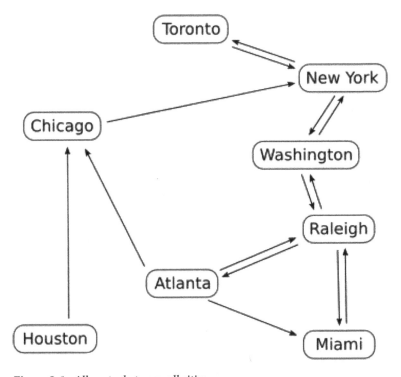

Figure 3-1. *All routes between all cities*

As you can see from looking at the routes, there are some loops in the paths. For example, Raleigh to Atlanta to Miami to Raleigh.

Let's say we want to find out all of the destinations we can get to from Raleigh. How would we do that using a CTE? Here's a proposed set of steps:

1. Look up all destinations from Raleigh.

2. Take those results and look up all their destinations.

3. Repeat until all destinations are found.

Step one looks to be perfect to use as our *<anchor>* part, with the other two steps being in the *<recursive>* part. The obvious *<anchor>* is to SELECT every route departing from Raleigh:

```
SELECT arriving FROM routes
WHERE departing='Raleigh';
```

This query gives us the following output:

```
+-------------+
| arriving    |
+-------------+
| Washington  |
| Atlanta     |
| Miami       |
+-------------+
```

For the *<recursive>* part of our CTE, we need to SELECT records with routes that have those cities as departing cities. We can do this by looking for arrivals from cities returned by our *<anchor>* as the initial departing cities and repeating the process until we have a list of all possible destinations.

Here's everything as a recursive CTE named destinations:

```
WITH RECURSIVE destinations AS (
    SELECT arriving
    FROM routes
    WHERE departing='Raleigh'
  UNION
    SELECT routes.arriving
    FROM destinations, routes
    WHERE
      destinations.arriving=routes.departing
)
SELECT * FROM destinations;
```

The results returned by this CTE are:

```
+------------+
| arriving   |
+------------+
| Washington |
| Atlanta    |
| Miami      |
| Chicago    |
| Raleigh    |
| New York   |
| Toronto    |
+------------+
```

As expected, the only city we can't get to from Raleigh is Houston. In fact, nobody can get to Houston by train because there's no path to Houston, only a single path out of Houston. We should lay some track and fix that.

Besides the absence of Houston, there are a couple things to note about this result. First is that Raleigh itself appears in the output, and the second is how the CTE was smart enough to not loop endlessly.

What provides closure to our CTE and prevents these loops from running until we hit @@max_recursive_iterations or @@max_statement_time is our use of UNION instead of UNION ALL. When UNION sees a duplicated result it ignores it, so once all possible cities have been located, the only cities being returned will be ones it has already seen, and so the CTE terminates.

What about the inclusion of Raleigh? Well, if you refer back to Figure 3-1, you'll see that from Raleigh there are several paths that lead back to Raleigh. All of the paths leaving Raleigh have paths that return to Raleigh; for example, Raleigh to Miami to Raleigh. There is also a big circle of Raleigh to Atlanta to Chicago to New York to Washington back to Raleigh. Because Raleigh wasn't in our list to begin with, it is included in the result like any other valid destination, but only once. Any additional times Raleigh appears in new results it will be ignored.

If we want to remove Raleigh from our result, we can simply change the final line to:

```
SELECT * FROM destinations WHERE arriving!='Raleigh';
```

We could, alternatively, move Raleigh to the first position of our results, which makes a bit more sense logically. After all, the first location we can get to is where we are right now. To do this, we need to cheat a little and tell the parser that we're selecting Raleigh as an arrival even though we're actually selecting it as departing city. The SQL looks like this:

```
SELECT departing AS arriving
  FROM routes
  WHERE departing='Raleigh';
```

Running this query by itself gives us the following:

```
+----------+
| arriving |
+----------+
| Raleigh  |
| Raleigh  |
| Raleigh  |
+----------+
```

This result is expected because there are three routes from Raleigh to other cities. We can now plug this into our CTE to get the following:

```
WITH RECURSIVE destinations AS (
    SELECT departing AS arriving
    FROM routes
    WHERE departing='Raleigh'
  UNION
    SELECT routes.arriving
    FROM destinations, routes
    WHERE
      destinations.arriving=routes.departing
)
SELECT * FROM destinations;
```

And the result is:

```
+------------+
| arriving   |
+------------+
| Raleigh    |
| Washington |
| Atlanta    |
| Miami      |
| Chicago    |
| New York   |
| Toronto    |
+------------+
```

This still gives us Raleigh in the output, but at least it is the first result instead of it confusingly showing up in the middle of the results.

Finding All Possible Paths

Finding all of the possible destinations we can get to from Raleigh is nice, but what about finding all of the possible paths we could take to get from Raleigh to every city we can get to from Raleigh?

Here are the steps to do this:

1.   Look up destinations from our starting point.

2.   Find destinations from that point and add them; UNION will prevent duplicates.

3.   Repeat until all possible paths are found.

Because we want to start from Raleigh, for our *<anchor>* we need to do something similar to what we did in the previous section and issue our SELECT in such a way that it starts from Raleigh. Here's a possible *<anchor>* candidate:

```
SELECT departing, arriving
FROM routes
  WHERE departing='Raleigh';
```

This gives us what we would expect:

```
+-----------+------------+
| departing | arriving   |
+-----------+------------+
| Raleigh   | Washington |
| Raleigh   | Atlanta    |
| Raleigh   | Miami      |
+-----------+------------+
```

Our *<recursive>* part is going to be trickier. We want to show the complete set of every possible path, not just a list of end points. So, we therefore want to add any additions, if any, to a given path to the end of an existing path with a separator in between. The CONCAT() function was made for this sort of thing, and the departing column looks like the column we will want to concat on, because that's where our starting point, Raleigh, is.

After the first run-through of our *<recursive>* part, we should concat the departing and arriving columns together as our new departing column, and then also include our arriving column to use for the next run through the loop. We should end up with a result that outputs something that looks like this:

```
+----------------------+------------+
| departing            | arriving   |
+----------------------+------------+
| Raleigh > Washington | Washington |
| Raleigh > Atlanta    | Atlanta    |
| Raleigh > Miami      | Miami      |
+----------------------+------------+
```

Actually, the departing column name doesn't make sense, because it is holding our path, not the initial departure city, so let's call it *path* in our actual CTE.

Are we now ready to actually write our CTE? Actually, not quite! There's one other issue we should solve first. Look again at Figure 3-1; what can we do to prevent silly results like the following?

```
Raleigh > Washington > New York > Washington > Raleigh > Miami
```

This is a perfectly valid path, but it isn't one that any sane person would take. If we want to go from Raleigh to Miami, we would take that route; we would never go to New York first then back through Raleigh to Miami. What can we do to prevent this? The LOCATE() function provides an easy way. It searches a string for a given substring, returning 0 if the substring is not found. So, all we need to do is add something like the following to the WHERE clause of our *<recursive>* part:

```
LOCATE(routes.arriving, <cte_name>.paths)=0
```

We will, of course, replace *<cte_name>* with the actual name of our CTE.

Let's try putting everything together, finally, into a CTE named full_routes:

```
WITH RECURSIVE full_routes AS (
    SELECT departing AS path, arriving
    FROM routes
    WHERE departing='Raleigh'
  UNION
    SELECT
      CONCAT(full_routes.path, ' > ',
             routes.arriving),
      routes.arriving
    FROM full_routes, routes
    WHERE
      full_routes.arriving=routes.departing
      AND
      LOCATE(routes.arriving, full_routes.path)=0
) SELECT * FROM full_routes;
```

This CTE looks reasonable, but when we run it, the result is obviously wrong:

```
+--------------------------------------------+------------+
| path                                       | arriving   |
+--------------------------------------------+------------+
| Raleigh                                    | Washington |
| Raleigh                                    | Atlanta    |
| Raleigh                                    | Miami      |
| Raleigh > Chicago                          | Chicago    |
| Raleigh > New York                         | New York   |
| Raleigh > Miami                            | Miami      |
| Raleigh > Chicago > New York               | New York   |
| Raleigh > New York > Washington            | Washington |
| Raleigh > New York > Toronto               | Toronto    |
| Raleigh > Chicago > New York > Washington  | Washington |
| Raleigh > Chicago > New York > Toronto     | Toronto    |
+--------------------------------------------+------------+
```

What is going on here? Where are our expected *Raleigh > Washington, Raleigh > Atlanta*, and *Raleigh > Miami* paths? And there's no way to get directly from Raleigh to Chicago, as you need to go through Washington first. Actually, the same is true with all of the paths; they're all missing one stop.

If we look closer at the logic of our recursive CTE, the reason becomes clear.

During the first run-through of our *<recursive>* part, our WHERE clause is looking for cities in the arriving column that also appear in the departing column of the routes table. During the initial loop through the result set, our recursive CTE has access to only what was returned by our *<anchor>* part, the three cities Washington, Atlanta, and Miami. As we asked it to, our recursive CTE first looks for a row in the routes table that has *Washington* in the departing column, and the first result it finds is the Washington to Chicago entry. It then dutifully concats *Chicago* to the value in the path column, which is *Raleigh*, as a new result row. That's why the fourth row of our output is:

```
+-------------------+----------+
| path              | arriving |
+-------------------+----------+
| Raleigh > Chicago | Chicago  |
+-------------------+----------+
```

To fix this, we need to somehow set our *<anchor>* so that our starting point is just Raleigh. Then, during the first run-through it will correctly concat Washington, Atlanta, and Miami to the path. What if instead of our *<anchor>* returning Raleigh's actual connections, we just select the departing column again and tell the CTE that it is the arriving column? It seems a bit cheaty, but the SQL for it is perfectly valid:

```
SELECT departing AS path, departing AS arriving
  FROM routes
  WHERE departing='Raleigh';
```

Importantly, the result of this query contains a result that should work perfectly fine as our *<anchor>*:

```
+---------+----------+
| path    | arriving |
+---------+----------+
| Raleigh | Raleigh  |
| Raleigh | Raleigh  |
| Raleigh | Raleigh  |
+---------+----------+
```

After putting our new *<anchor>* into our full_routes CTE, it now looks like this:

```
WITH RECURSIVE full_routes AS (
    SELECT departing AS path, departing AS arriving
    FROM routes
    WHERE departing='Raleigh'
  UNION
```

```
SELECT
  CONCAT(full_routes.path, ' > ',
         routes.arriving),
  routes.arriving
FROM full_routes, routes
WHERE
  full_routes.arriving=routes.departing
  AND
  LOCATE(routes.arriving, full_routes.path)=0
) SELECT * FROM full_routes;
```

And the result is what we would expect:

```
+--------------------------------------------------------+------------+
| path                                                   | arriving   |
+--------------------------------------------------------+------------+
| Raleigh                                                | Raleigh    |
| Raleigh > Washington                                   | Washington |
| Raleigh > Atlanta                                      | Atlanta    |
| Raleigh > Miami                                        | Miami      |
| Raleigh > Atlanta > Chicago                            | Chicago    |
| Raleigh > Washington > New York                        | New York   |
| Raleigh > Atlanta > Miami                              | Miami      |
| Raleigh > Atlanta > Chicago > New York                 | New York   |
| Raleigh > Washington > New York > Toronto              | Toronto    |
| Raleigh > Atlanta > Chicago > New York > Washington    | Washington |
| Raleigh > Atlanta > Chicago > New York > Toronto       | Toronto    |
+--------------------------------------------------------+------------+
```

The first result is a little silly, with both the path and arriving columns as Raleigh, but the rest of the results are exactly what we would expect. And, actually, the next time I need to take the train from Raleigh to Washington, I should take the scenic route and get there via Atlanta, Chicago, and New York.

Just for fun, I removed the LOCATE part of the WHERE clause to see how many possible non-duplicated combinations there were. On MySQL 8.0.2 DMR it returned an error:

```
ERROR 1406 (22001): Data too long for column 'path' at row 231
```

However, on MariaDB 10.2 it returned all of the possible combinations. There are a lot. Appropriately, for Dragon Ball Z fans, it's *over 9000*!

9117 to be exact.

Summary

In this chapter, we explored how recursive CTEs differ from non-recursive CTEs. We explored a few of their many uses:

- Solving recursive math problems
- Walking a genealogical tree to match children with their ancestors
- Finding all possible routes between two points

There are many more uses, but we're going to switch gears for the next three chapters so that we can explore the second major topic of this book, Window Functions. We'll then return to CTEs and combine them with Window Functions in Chapter 7, because, why not?

PART II

Window Functions

CHAPTER 4

■ ■ ■

Basics of Window Functions

The first three chapters have all been about CTEs. For this and the next two chapters, we are switching gears and will be exploring Window Functions. Like CTEs, these were introduced in MariaDB 10.2 and MySQL 8.0 (as of 8.0.2 DMR).

At its core, a Window Function is like any other function; it operates on the data in the database to manipulate it in a useful way. The primary syntactic difference is that Window Functions are used with a custom SQL keyword, OVER. Practically, they can do things other functions can only dream of. This chapter will familiarize you with the basic syntax and provide a quick overview of all the various Window Functions.

What Is a function?

In general computer programming terms, a function can be thought of as a subprogram of your main program. Its logic is isolated from the main program and is referenced or called whenever it is needed.

MariaDB and MySQL contain many useful built-in functions that can do a variety of things. There are functions like LOWER, CONCAT, SUBSTR, and others, which help manipulate strings of text. There are functions such as ABS, LOG, ROUND, and others, which help perform various mathematical operations. There are also aggregate functions like SUM, AVG, MAX, and others, which help perform actions on groups of rows. And there are other functions for working with dates, XML, JSON, GIS, and other types of data.

Window Functions are a new class of function. When you use a regular function, you have access to the data from the current row and produce one result for each row in the result set. When you use an aggregate function, you can compute one result from the group of rows in the result set. Window Functions can do both of these tasks. They are computed over a range of rows, but they can also give you results for each row.

D. Bartholomew, *MariaDB and MySQL Common Table Expressions and Window Functions Revealed*, https://doi.org/10.1007/978-1-4842-3120-3_4

Window Function Syntax

As mentioned previously, the keyword to look for to identify Window Functions is OVER. The basic syntax for calling a Window Function within a SELECT statement is:

```
<function_name>([<expression>]) OVER (
  [<partition_definition>]
  [<order_definition>]
  [<frame_definition>]
)
...
[<WINDOW_clause>]
```

Inside the OVER clause are three possible optional elements, *<partition_definition>*, *<order_definition>*, and *<frame_definition>*. We'll cover each of them separately.

The opening and closing parentheses after OVER are mandatory, unless the optional WINDOW clause is used, even if no *partition*, *order*, or *frame* definitions are set. See the "WINDOW Clause Syntax" section for more information.

Partition Definition Syntax

The *<partition_definition>* section syntax looks like the following:

```
PARTITION BY <expression>[{,<expression>}...]
```

The *<partition_definition>* section is supported by all Window Functions. Its purpose is to restrict the rows a given function operates on to a specific set within the full result set.

The *<expression>* part can be any valid expression such as would be used in the GROUP BY section of a traditional query. Multiple expressions can be specified, separated by commas.

Order Definition Syntax

The *<order_definition>* section syntax looks like the following:

```
ORDER BY <expression> [ASC|DESC] [{,<expression>}...]
```

The *<order_definition>* section is supported by all Window Functions. Its purpose is to set the order of the results as seen by the function itself as the Window Function runs prior to any outside ORDER BY clause in the full query.

The *<expression>* part can be any valid SQL expression as used in the ORDER BY section of a traditional query. Results can also be ordered in ascending (ASC) or descending (DESC) order. Multiple expressions can be specified, separated by commas.

Frame Definition Syntax

The *<frame_definition>* section syntax looks like the following:

```
{ROWS|RANGE}
  {<frame_start>|<frame_between>}
```

The *<frame_definition>* section is not supported by all Window Functions. Its purpose is to define a frame that is then used by the function to compute a result on the rows in the frame. The frame moves with the current row. In addition to its own defined boundaries, the frame is further bounded by the *<partition_definition>* section.

The *<frame_definition>* section is the most powerful feature of Window Functions. The next chapter contains several fully worked examples that show how frame-moving works.

There are two basic parts to a *<frame_definition>*. First, you specify either ROWS or RANGE, and you then specify the boundary of your frame using a *<frame_start>* or *<frame_between>* section.

A *<frame_start>* section contains one of the following:

- UNBOUNDED PRECEDING

- <expression> PRECEDING

- CURRENT ROW

A *<frame_between>* section is a little more complicated. It contains:

```
BETWEEN <frame_boundary1> AND <frame_boundary2>
```

The *<frame_boundary1>* and *<frame_boundary2>* sections can each contain one of the following:

- <frame_start>

- UNBOUNDED FOLLOWING

- <expression> FOLLOWING

If this seems a little complicated, don't worry. After a little experience with writing *<frame_definition>* sections, it becomes second nature.

Another way of looking at the entire syntax of a *<frame_definition>* all at once is by using Extended Backus Naur Form (EBNF) notation. In EBNF notation, the syntax looks like this:

```
frame_definition ::= ( ROWS | RANGE ) (
  CURRENT ROW
  | ( UNBOUNDED | 'value_expr' ) PRECEDING
  | ( BETWEEN (
        UNBOUNDED PRECEDING
        | CURRENT ROW
        | 'value_expr' (PREDEDING|FOLLOWING)
```

43

```
   )
   AND (
      UNBOUNDED FOLLOWING
      | CURRENT ROW
      | 'value_expr' (PRECEDING | FOLLOWING)
   )
  )
)
```

There are online tools, such as those found at `http://bottlecaps.de/rr/ui`, that can convert EBNF into a railroad diagram that even better visualizes the syntax. Figure 4-1 shows a railroad diagram for the complete *<frame_definition>* syntax.

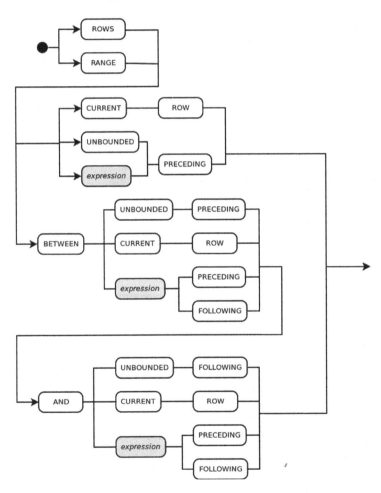

***Figure 4-1.** Railroad diagram of the <frame_definition> syntax*

Railroad diagrams are useful because you can just follow the paths from one element to the next, like a train traveling along railroad tracks, choosing the branch you want to follow when the path forks.

Putting it all together, here are some examples of valid *<frame_definition>* sections:

```
ROWS UNBOUNDED PRECEDING
ROWS CURRENT ROW
ROWS 3 PRECEDING
ROWS BETWEEN CURRENT ROW AND UNBOUNDED FOLLOWING
RANGE BETWEEN 1 PRECEDING AND CURRENT ROW
ROWS BETWEEN CURRENT ROW AND 5 PRECEDING
```

■ **Tip**   Some combinations may seem possible, based on the rules in the syntax definition, but are not allowed. For example, using a *<frame_definition>* like this:

```
ROWS BETWEEN 3 FOLLOWING AND CURRENT ROW
```

will result in the following error:

```
ERROR 4014 (HY000): Unacceptable combination of window frame bound
specifications
```

The solution here is to just switch the two boundary definitions around and do this instead:

```
ROWS BETWEEN CURRENT ROW AND 3 FOLLOWING
```

See the entry on the SUM( ) function later in this chapter for a brief look at how window frames work in practice. We'll also be exploring them in greater depth in the following chapters.

WINDOW Clause Syntax

An alternative to the OVER definition in a Window Function is to use a WINDOW clause between the FROM and ORDER BY clauses of our SELECT statement. The syntax of a WINDOW clause is as follows:

```
WINDOW <window_name> AS (
  [<partition_definition>]
  [<order_definition>]
  [<frame_definition>]
)[, <window_name> AS (...)]...
```

When using a `WINDOW` clause, replace the `()` after `OVER` in your Window Function, including everything that would have been inside it, with *<window_name>*.

Here's a hypothetical example:

```
SELECT
  office, time, amount,
  SUM(amount)OVER window1
FROM my_table
  WINDOW window1 AS (
    PARTITION BY office
    ORDER BY time)
ORDER BY office,time;
```

The purpose of the `WINDOW` clause is to help keep the part of the `SELECT` statement between `SELECT` and `FROM` cleaner and easier to read. It also helps avoid duplication in cases where multiple Window Functions are used that have similar `OVER` clauses.

If multiple *<window_name>* sections are defined, the later ones are able to inherit from previous ones. For example:

```
WINDOW
  window1 AS (PARTITION BY id),
  window2 AS (window1 ORDER BY office),
  window3 AS (window2 ROWS UNBOUNDED PRECEDING)
```

So `window2` will effectively be:

```
(PARTITION BY id ORDER BY office)
```

And `window3` will effectively be:

```
(
  PARTITION BY id
  ORDER BY office
  ROWS UNBOUNDED PRECEDING
)
```

The order of how you add *<window_name>* sections must follow the rules for `OVER` clauses. First, the *<partition_definition>*, then the *<order_definition>*, and last of all the *<frame_definition>*.

It's also worth noting that a `WINDOW` subclause can only inherit a maximum of one other `WINDOW` subclause in its definition. For example, you may logically think the following would be valid:

```
WINDOW
  window1 AS (PARTITION BY id),
  window2 AS (ORDER BY office),
  window3 AS (window1 window2 ROWS UNBOUNDED PRECEDING)
```

But trying to do it would give you an error message.

See Chapter 6 for an example of using the WINDOW clause to simplify a query.

Window Functions Reference

To familiarize you with all of the available Window Functions in MariaDB and MySQL, the rest of this chapter will go over each of them and their syntax.

This section is meant to be used as a reference when looking up a specific Window Function. It is not necessarily meant to be read straight through, though you can (and probably should) do that at least once.

Some Window Functions don't exist in any form as a non-Window Function, so they are wholly new. Others already existed in MariaDB or MySQL prior to the introduction of Window Functions as aggregate functions, like AVG. So, while you may have seen and used them before, they have a special Window Function form when called with an OVER clause. The functions are listed alphabetically to make them easier to look up.

Window Functions are available in MariaDB 10.2 and in MySQL 8.0 as of the MySQL 8.0.2 DMR.

AVG()

The AVG aggregate function can be used as a Window Function if the OVER clause is included. The syntax is:

```
AVG(<expression>) OVER (
  [<partition_definition>]
  [<order_definition>]
  [<frame_definition>]
)
```

The AVG function returns the average of *<expres sion>* as viewed by the OVER clause.

BIT_AND()

The BIT_AND aggregate function can be used as a Window Function if the OVER clause is included. The syntax is:

```
BIT_AND(<expression>) OVER (
  [<partition_definition>]
  [<order_definition>]
  [<frame_definition>]
)
```

The BIT_AND function returns the bitwise AND of the bits of *<expression>* as viewed by the OVER clause.

BIT_OR()

The BIT_OR aggregate function can be used as a Window Function if the OVER clause is included. The syntax is:

```
BIT_OR(<expression>) OVER (
  [<partition_definition>]
  [<order_definition>]
  [<frame_definition>]
)
```

The BIT_OR function returns the bitwise OR of the bits of *<expression>* as viewed by the OVER clause.

BIT_XOR()

The BIT_XOR aggregate function can be used as a Window Function if the OVER clause is included. The syntax is:

```
BIT_XOR(<expression>) OVER (
  [<partition_definition>]
  [<order_definition>]
  [<frame_definition>]
)
```

The BIT_XOR function returns the bitwise XOR (exclusive OR) of the bits of *<expression>* as viewed by the OVER clause.

COUNT()

The COUNT aggregate function can be used as a Window Function if the OVER clause is included. The syntax is:

```
COUNT(<expression>) OVER (
  [<partition_definition>]
  [<order_definition>]
  [<frame_definition>]
)
```

The COUNT function returns a count of the number of non-NULL values of *<expression>* as viewed by the OVER clause.

CUME_DIST()

The syntax for the CUME_DIST function is:

```
CUME_DIST() OVER (
  [ <partition_definition> ]
  [ <order_definition> ]
)
```

The CUME_DIST function returns the cumulative distribution of a row. The value is calculated using the following formula:

```
(number of rows <= current row) / (total rows)
```

For example, when using CUME_DIST on the values '1,2,2,3,4' the results would be as follows:

```
+-------+--------------+
| value | cume_dist    |
+-------+--------------+
|     1 | 0.2000000000 |
|     2 | 0.6000000000 |
|     2 | 0.6000000000 |
|     3 | 0.8000000000 |
|     4 | 1.0000000000 |
+-------+--------------+
```

DENSE_RANK()

The syntax for the DENSE_RANK function is:

```
DENSE_RANK() OVER (
  [ <partition_definition> ]
  [ <order_definition> ]
)
```

The DENSE_RANK function displays a number for a given row, beginning with 1, and following the *<order_definition>* and *<partition_definition>* sections. Identical values are given the same result. Unlike the RANK function, the DENSE_RANK function does not skip numbers when it resumes numbering results following giving identical values to the same result.

For example, when using DENSE_RANK on the values '1,2,2,3,4' the results would be:

```
+-------+------------+
| value | dense_rank |
+-------+------------+
|     1 |          1 |
|     2 |          2 |
|     2 |          2 |
|     3 |          3 |
|     4 |          4 |
+-------+------------+
```

Because DENSE_RANK doesn't skip values, the result ends up being identical to the value column.

FIRST_VALUE()

The syntax for the FIRST_VALUE function is:

```
FIRST_VALUE(<expression>) OVER (
  [ <partition_definition> ]
  [ <order_definition> ]
)
```

The FIRST_VALUE function returns the first row of the results as viewed by the OVER clause.

LAG()

The syntax for the LAG function is:

```
LAG(<expression>[,<offset>][,<default>]) OVER (
  [ <partition_definition> ]
  [ <order_definition> ]
)
```

The LAG function returns the value of *expression* offset by the given *offset* amount *before* the current row. If the value is NULL, it can optionally return a *default* value instead. If *offset* is not specified, it defaults to 1.

The *default* argument is only available on MySQL 8.0.2 or later; it is not yet available in MariaDB as of MariaDB 10.2.8.

LAST_VALUE()

The syntax for the LAST_VALUE function is:

```
LAST_VALUE(<expression>) OVER (
  [ <partition_definition> ]
  [ <order_definition> ]
)
```

The LAST_VALUE function returns the last row of the results as viewed by the OVER clause.

LEAD()

The syntax for the LEAD function is:

```
LEAD(<expression>[,<offset>][,<default>]) OVER (
  [ <partition_definition> ]
  [ <order_definition> ]
)
```

The LEAD function returns the value of *<expression>* offset by the given *<offset>* amount *after* the current row. If the value is NULL, it can optionally return a *<default>* value instead. If *<offset>* is not specified it defaults to 1.

The *<default>* argument is only available on MySQL 8.0.2 or later; it is not yet available in MariaDB as of MariaDB 10.2.8.

NTH_VALUE()

The syntax for the NTH_VALUE function is:

```
NTH_VALUE(<expression>, <nth_expression>) OVER (
  [ <partition_definition> ]
  [ <order_definition> ]
)
```

The NTH_VALUE function returns the value that is the nth row of the result as defined in the OVER clause.

For example, if we have a table with two columns, key and a, which have the following values:

```
+-----+------+
| key | a    |
+-----+------+
|   1 |    0 |
|   2 |    0 |
|   3 |    0 |
|   4 |    1 |
|   5 |    1 |
|   6 |    1 |
|   7 |    2 |
|   8 |    2 |
|   9 |    2 |
|  10 |    2 |
|  11 |    2 |
+-----+------+
```

if we call NTH_VALUE(key, a + 1) OVER (PARTITION BY a ORDER BY key)AS a1 the result is as follows:

```
+-----+------+------+
| key | a    | a1   |
+-----+------+------+
|   1 |   0  |   1  |
|   2 |   0  |   1  |
|   3 |   0  |   1  |
|   4 |   1  | NULL |
|   5 |   1  |   5  |
|   6 |   1  |   5  |
|   7 |   2  | NULL |
|   8 |   2  | NULL |
|   9 |   2  |   9  |
|  10 |   2  |   9  |
|  11 |   2  |   9  |
+-----+------+------+
```

Because we are partitioning on column a, the function evaluates based only on the rows in that partition. So, at row 4, the offset *a + 1* equals *2*, but because the function hasn't processed row 5 yet there is no value for the second row of that partition, so the value returned is NULL. The same thing happens with the third partition, only in that case the *<nth_expression>* equals 3 so it takes until the third row is processed before a non-NULL result is returned.

NTILE

The syntax for the NTILE function is:

```
NTILE (<ntile_expression>) OVER (
  [ <partition_definition> ]
  [ <order_definition> ]
)
```

This function returns an integer indicating the group a certain row is in. The number of groups is specified by the *<ntile_expression>* part, and the numbering starts at 1. Ordered rows in the partition are divided into the specified number of groups, with each group being as equal in size to the other groups as possible.

For example, when using NTILE(2) on the values '1,2,2,3,4' the results would be:

```
+-------+----------+
| value | ntile(2) |
+-------+----------+
|     1 |        1 |
|     2 |        1 |
|     2 |        1 |
|     3 |        2 |
|     4 |        2 |
+-------+----------+
```

And the result using NTILE(3) on those same values would be:

```
+-------+----------+
| value | ntile(3) |
+-------+----------+
|     1 |        1 |
|     2 |        1 |
|     2 |        2 |
|     3 |        2 |
|     4 |        3 |
+-------+----------+
```

PERCENT_RANK()

The syntax for the PERCENT_RANK function is:

```
PERCENT_RANK() OVER (
  [ <partition_definition> ]
  [ <order_definition> ]
)
```

The PERCENT_RANK function returns the relative percent rank of a given row. The formula used to calculate the percent rank is:

```
(rank - 1) / (number of rows in the window or partition - 1)
```

For example, when using PERCENT_RANK on the values '1,2,2,3,4' the results would be:

```
+-------+--------------+
| value | percent_rank |
+-------+--------------+
|     1 | 0.0000000000 |
|     2 | 0.2500000000 |
|     2 | 0.2500000000 |
|     3 | 0.7500000000 |
|     4 | 1.0000000000 |
+-------+--------------+
```

RANK()

The syntax for the RANK function is:

```
RANK() OVER (
  [ <partition_definition> ]
  [ <order_definition> ]
)
```

The RANK function displays a number for a given row, beginning with 1, and following the <order_definition> and <partition_definition> sections. Identical values are given the same result, with numbering resuming at the next non-identical result, skipping values.

For example, when using RANK on the values '1,2,2,3,4' the results would be:

```
+-------+------+
| value | rank |
+-------+------+
|     1 |    1 |
|     2 |    2 |
|     2 |    2 |
|     3 |    4 |
|     4 |    5 |
+-------+------+
```

Because RANK skips values, the result skips the third rank and jumps to the fourth when it resumes ranking after the two rows where *value=2*.

ROW_NUMBER()

The syntax for the ROW_NUMBER function is:

```
ROW_NUMBER() OVER (
  [ <partition_definition> ]
  [ <order_definition> ]
)
```

The ROW_NUMBER() function is similar to the RANK() and DENSE_RANK() functions, but where those functions will assign the same number to matching rows based on ORDER BY, the ROW_NUMBER function always increases the count for every row.

For example, when using ROW_NUMBER on the values '1,2,2,3,4' the results would be:

```
+-------+------------+
| value | row_number |
+-------+------------+
|     1 |          1 |
|     2 |          2 |
|     2 |          3 |
|     3 |          4 |
|     4 |          5 |
+-------+------------+
```

SUM()

The SUM aggregate function can be used as a Window Function if the OVER clause is included. The syntax is:

```
SUM(<expression>) OVER (
  [<partition_definition>]
  [<order_definition>]
  [<frame_definition>]
)
```

The SUM function returns the sum of the rows from *<expression>* as viewed by the OVER clause.

As an example of how Window Functions like SUM work with *<frame_definition>* sections, here is a brief example. Given a table, my_table, with a column, value, that contains the values 1,2,2,3,4, we can use the SUM function to easily add the current row with the previous two rows, if any, like so:

```
SELECT value,
  SUM(value) OVER (
    ORDER BY value
    ROWS
      BETWEEN 2 PRECEDING AND CURRENT ROW
    ) AS sum
FROM my_table
ORDER BY value;
```

The result of the preceding query is:

```
+-------+------+
| value | sum  |
+-------+------+
|     1 | 1    |
|     2 | 3    |
|     2 | 5    |
|     3 | 7    |
|     4 | 9    |
+-------+------+
```

Let's step through the result line by line.

For line 1, the value is *1*, and there are no previous rows, so the frame the SUM function is looking at only contains the first line of the result, which is *1*.

For line 2, the value is *2*, and there is one previous row, so the frame the SUM function is looking at only contains lines 1 and 2, or *(1+2)*, or *3*.

For line 3, the value is *2*, and there are two previous rows, so the frame the SUM function is looking at contains lines 1, 2, and 3 of the result, or *1+2+2*, or *5*.

For line 4, the value is *3*, and there are three previous rows, but the frame only contains the current row and the previous two rows, so the lines the SUM function is looking at contains lines 2, 3, and 4, or *(2+2+3)*, or *7*.

Line 5 is calculated the same way as for line 4, but the values being added together are *(2+3+4)*, or *9*.

Summary

In this chapter, we covered the basic syntax of Window Functions, breaking them down into their component parts and then going through each part separately. We also went through all of the available Window Functions, describing each one and what they are used for, with simple examples where appropriate to illustrate how they work. We'll cover more examples in the following chapters, including demonstrating frames and how they are used.

CHAPTER 5

■ ■ ■

Recognizing Opportunities for Window Functions

The previous chapter was an overview of what Window Functions are, with details on the syntax. It's time to put that knowledge into practice. This chapter expands upon that with some simple yet practical examples that illustrate some of the types of problems Window Functions are good at solving. We'll cover organizing results, maintaining running totals, and ranking results.

■ **Caution**   If you are using MySQL 8.0, you must be on at least version 8.0.2. This was the version that introduced Window Functions. Previous versions of MySQL, including MySQL 8.0.0 and 8.0.1, do not have Window Functions.

All versions of MariaDB 10.2 and higher have Window Functions.

Partitioning and Ordering Results

One of the most important purposes of a database is to organize the mountains of data that surround us. The *<partition_definition>* and *<order_definition>* sections of the OVER clause exist to help us do just that. We covered their syntax in the previous chapter, but some practical demonstrations of how these sections work is probably more useful than a dry syntax diagram on the path to mastering Window Functions.

Using the employees table from Chapter 1, here is a simple example of the ROW_ NUMBER Window Function. First, we'll call the function with none of the optional sections in the OVER clause:

```
SELECT
  ROW_NUMBER() OVER() AS rnum,
  name, title, office
FROM employees
WHERE office='Cleveland' OR office='Memphis'
ORDER BY title;
```

© Daniel Bartholomew 2017
D. Bartholomew, *MariaDB and MySQL Common Table Expressions and Window Functions Revealed*, https://doi.org/10.1007/978-1-4842-3120-3_5

The result is a little unexpected:

```
+------+-------------------+-------------+-----------+
| rnum | name              | title       | office    |
+------+-------------------+-------------+-----------+
|    1 | Eileen Morrow     | dba         | Cleveland |
|    3 | Douglas Williams  | dba         | Memphis   |
|    8 | Carol Monreal     | dba         | Cleveland |
|   14 | Elva Garcia       | dba         | Memphis   |
|    5 | Rosemary Bowers   | manager     | Cleveland |
|   12 | Richard Delgado   | manager     | Memphis   |
|    2 | Julius Ramos      | salesperson | Cleveland |
|    7 | Tammy Castro      | salesperson | Memphis   |
|    9 | Joyce Beck        | salesperson | Memphis   |
|   10 | Alonzo Page       | salesperson | Cleveland |
|   11 | Tina Jefferson    | salesperson | Cleveland |
|   13 | Leo Gutierrez     | salesperson | Cleveland |
|   15 | Joann Smith       | salesperson | Memphis   |
|    4 | Janet Edwards     | support     | Memphis   |
|    6 | Louise Lewis      | support     | Cleveland |
+------+-------------------+-------------+-----------+
```

Looking at this result, you might be confused as to why the rnum column is out of order. In fact, your result may have a different rnum column entirely. It may be in order from 1 to 15, or it may have a completely different order. What is going on? The out-of-order rnum column happens because Window Functions are computed *after* the other parts of the SELECT statement have been fetched (the name, title, and office columns in our example) and after any WHERE, HAVING, or GROUP BY clauses, but before the final ORDER BY title clause. In fact, without an <order_definition> section in the OVER clause, Window Functions do not guarantee any particular ordering.

Ideally, we want the rnum column to always match the end output of the ORDER BY title clause. To ensure this happens, we add an <order_definition> section to the OVER clause like so:

```
SELECT
  ROW_NUMBER()
    OVER (
      ORDER BY title
    ) AS rnum,
  name, title, office
FROM employees
WHERE office='Cleveland' OR office='Memphis'
ORDER BY title;
```

Now both the rnum column and the final output are guaranteed to be ordered by the contents of the title column, so the result will always make logical sense:

```
+------+-------------------+-------------+-----------+
| rnum | name              | title       | office    |
+------+-------------------+-------------+-----------+
|    1 | Eileen Morrow     | dba         | Cleveland |
|    2 | Douglas Williams  | dba         | Memphis   |
|    3 | Carol Monreal     | dba         | Cleveland |
|    4 | Elva Garcia       | dba         | Memphis   |
|    5 | Rosemary Bowers   | manager     | Cleveland |
|    6 | Richard Delgado   | manager     | Memphis   |
|    7 | Julius Ramos      | salesperson | Cleveland |
|    8 | Tammy Castro      | salesperson | Memphis   |
|    9 | Joyce Beck        | salesperson | Memphis   |
|   10 | Alonzo Page       | salesperson | Cleveland |
|   11 | Tina Jefferson    | salesperson | Cleveland |
|   12 | Leo Gutierrez     | salesperson | Cleveland |
|   13 | Joann Smith       | salesperson | Memphis   |
|   14 | Janet Edwards     | support     | Memphis   |
|   15 | Louise Lewis      | support     | Cleveland |
+------+-------------------+-------------+-----------+
```

Between the Cleveland and Memphis offices there are 15 employees. What if we want to number employees in separate offices, well, separately?

This is the purpose of the *<partition_definition>* section. It allows us to group our results. With a *<partition_definition>* section in the OVER clause, the ROW_NUMBER function will do its thing to each group independently. So, we'll add PARTITION BY office to the OVER clause like so:

```
SELECT
  ROW_NUMBER() OVER (
    PARTITION by office
    ORDER BY title
  ) AS rnum,
  name, title, office
FROM employees
WHERE office='Cleveland' OR office='Memphis'
ORDER BY title;
```

Unfortunately, the output is not as useful as we might have supposed:

```
+------+------------------+-------------+-----------+
| rnum | name             | title       | office    |
+------+------------------+-------------+-----------+
|    1 | Eileen Morrow    | dba         | Cleveland |
|    1 | Douglas Williams | dba         | Memphis   |
|    2 | Carol Monreal    | dba         | Cleveland |
|    2 | Elva Garcia      | dba         | Memphis   |
|    3 | Rosemary Bowers  | manager     | Cleveland |
|    3 | Richard Delgado  | manager     | Memphis   |
|    4 | Julius Ramos     | salesperson | Cleveland |
|    4 | Tammy Castro     | salesperson | Memphis   |
|    5 | Joyce Beck       | salesperson | Memphis   |
|    5 | Alonzo Page      | salesperson | Cleveland |
|    6 | Tina Jefferson   | salesperson | Cleveland |
|    7 | Leo Gutierrez    | salesperson | Cleveland |
|    6 | Joann Smith      | salesperson | Memphis   |
|    7 | Janet Edwards    | support     | Memphis   |
|    8 | Louise Lewis     | support     | Cleveland |
+------+------------------+-------------+-----------+
```

As with other results in this chapter, yours may be slightly different from this. But the <partition_definition> section is working perfectly here. The first Cleveland and first Memphis employees in the result are both given a row number of 1. The second ones 2, and so on. There's a little confusion further down in the results because Cleveland has more salespersons than Memphis, but the correct row numbers are all there. We just need to fix the output so that it is more understandable.

This is another instance that plainly shows that Window Functions do not guarantee ordering. The solution in our case is to just add the office column, not in the OVER clause, but to the final ORDER BY clause, before title, like so:

```
SELECT
  ROW_NUMBER() OVER (
    PARTITION by office
    ORDER BY title
  ) AS rnum,
  name, title, office
FROM employees
WHERE office='Cleveland' OR office='Memphis'
ORDER BY office,title;
```

The output now looks like this:

```
+------+--------------------+-------------+-----------+
| rnum | name               | title       | office    |
+------+--------------------+-------------+-----------+
|    1 | Eileen Morrow      | dba         | Cleveland |
|    2 | Carol Monreal      | dba         | Cleveland |
|    3 | Rosemary Bowers    | manager     | Cleveland |
|    4 | Julius Ramos       | salesperson | Cleveland |
|    5 | Alonzo Page        | salesperson | Cleveland |
|    6 | Tina Jefferson     | salesperson | Cleveland |
|    7 | Leo Gutierrez      | salesperson | Cleveland |
|    8 | Louise Lewis       | support     | Cleveland |
|    1 | Douglas Williams   | dba         | Memphis   |
|    2 | Elva Garcia        | dba         | Memphis   |
|    3 | Richard Delgado    | manager     | Memphis   |
|    4 | Tammy Castro       | salesperson | Memphis   |
|    5 | Joyce Beck         | salesperson | Memphis   |
|    6 | Joann Smith        | salesperson | Memphis   |
|    7 | Janet Edwards      | support     | Memphis   |
+------+--------------------+-------------+-----------+
```

Success! Each office's employees are numbered independently, and the numbering is all in order.

Maintaining a Running Total

Another common database task is to maintain a running total of something. This could be an account balance, the number of items sold over a period of months, or a host of other numeric values.

The commissions table we used back in Chapter 2 can be used to demonstrate this. It tracks commissions from salespersons in our fictional company. The table records the salesperson's ID number, an ID number for the commission, the commission amount, and the date of the commission.

A brief sample of the data can be seen with the following query:

```
SELECT
  commission_date AS date,
  salesperson_id as sp,
  commission_id as id,
  commission_amount as amount
FROM commissions
ORDER BY sp,date;
```

The complete output is quite long, but here's the first ten rows of output:

```
+-------------+----+-------+--------+
| date        | sp | id    | amount |
+-------------+----+-------+--------+
| 2016-01-21  | 3  | 15165 | 429.50 |
| 2016-02-09  | 3  | 15231 | 142.37 |
| 2016-02-12  | 3  | 15253 | 184.74 |
| 2016-03-22  | 3  | 15428 | 169.62 |
| 2016-04-01  | 3  | 15476 | 363.53 |
| 2016-05-10  | 3  | 15644 | 358.49 |
| 2016-07-11  | 3  | 15901 | 149.64 |
| 2016-11-25  | 3  | 16465 | 452.04 |
| 2017-01-25  | 3  | 16726 | 145.68 |
| 2017-03-10  | 3  | 16927 | 216.16 |
...
+-------------+----+-------+--------+
```

To create a running commissions total, we need to take the first amount for a row matching a given salesperson and output it in a column. We'll call this column total. Then, for each subsequent row we add the previous total to the current row's commission and make that the new total and so on until we come to a new salesperson_id, whereupon we will start the process over. At least, that's my way of thinking through the problem. Actually solving this using traditional SQL is a bit different. For example, one traditional SQL way of solving the problem is to use a self-join and the SUM function like so:

```
SELECT
    commission_date AS date, salesperson_id as sp,
    commission_id as id, commission_amount as amount,
    (SELECT SUM(commission_amount)
      FROM commissions AS c2
      WHERE c2.salesperson_id = c1.salesperson_id AND
            c2.commission_date <= c1.commission_date) AS total
FROM commissions AS c1
ORDER BY sp,date;
```

Inside our main query we have a subquery that looks for every row where the salesperson matches and the date is less than or equal to the date of the current row. For those rows that match the criteria, it sums them all up and outputs the answer in the total column. So, for the row with the oldest date stamp the only other row that it will match is itself, so the total column is the same as the commission_amount column for that row. For the row with the second oldest date stamp, the rows that match will be the oldest row and itself, so those are what are summed together into the total column. The process continues until all the rows that match a given salesperson_id have been fetched, and then the process restarts with the next salesperson.

The result is several thousand lines long, but here's the first few rows:

```
+------------+-----+-------+--------+----------+
| date       | sp  | id    | amount | total    |
+------------+-----+-------+--------+----------+
| 2016-01-21 |   3 | 15165 | 429.50 | 429.50   |
| 2016-02-09 |   3 | 15231 | 142.37 | 571.87   |
| 2016-02-12 |   3 | 15253 | 184.74 | 756.61   |
| 2016-03-22 |   3 | 15428 | 169.62 | 926.23   |
| 2016-04-01 |   3 | 15476 | 363.53 | 1289.76  |
| 2016-05-10 |   3 | 15644 | 358.49 | 1648.25  |
| 2016-07-11 |   3 | 15901 | 149.64 | 1797.89  |
| 2016-11-25 |   3 | 16465 | 452.04 | 2249.93  |
| 2017-01-25 |   3 | 16726 | 145.68 | 2395.61  |
| 2017-03-10 |   3 | 16927 | 216.16 | 2611.77  |
| 2017-04-05 |   3 | 17046 | 277.36 | 2889.13  |
| 2017-04-11 |   3 | 17072 | 151.36 | 3040.49  |
| 2017-05-29 |   3 | 17272 | 368.20 | 3408.69  |
...
+------------+-----+-------+--------+----------+
```

All in all, it works, and you could even say it works well. It's easy to confirm that the total column is accurately keeping a running total and that when the salesperson_id changes the count starts over.

But the process for how we get at the total is awkward. If this were a paper ledger, we wouldn't continuously re-add everything that came before; we would simply add the new value to the old total.

Also, all of the adding and re-adding our query is doing means we're constantly going out and fetching new groups of rows to sum together. All of this fetching and re-fetching takes time. Indexes can help, especially on large tables, but using a subquery like this doesn't seem like the right way to go about solving our original task of displaying a running total.

A Window Function can do this job much better, and it does it in a more natural way. First off, like our previous Window Function example where we were numbering employees, we need to use both the *<partition_definition>* and *<order_definition>* sections in our OVER clause. We'll PARTITION BY salesperson_id and ORDER BY commission_date to match the final ORDER BY clause of the query.

We then need to tell the Window Function what rows to add together for our total column. Aggregate Window Functions, like SUM, can use moving window frames to quickly identify the data they need to process. For this we'll use a *<frame_definition>* that goes from the beginning of our result set, or UNBOUNDED PRECEDING, to the CURRENT ROW, so our full *<frame_definition>* section will be:

ROWS BETWEEN UNBOUNDED PRECEDING AND CURRENT ROW

To put all of this in place, we take the previous query and replace the subquery part with our SUM Window Function, like so:

```
SELECT
  commission_date AS date, salesperson_id as sp,
  commission_id as id, commission_amount as amount,
  SUM(commission_amount)
    OVER (
      PARTITION BY salesperson_id
      ORDER BY commission_date
      ROWS BETWEEN UNBOUNDED PRECEDING AND CURRENT ROW
    ) AS total
FROM commissions AS c1
ORDER BY sp,date;
```

The result of this query is the same as we saw for the subquery version, so there's no need to show it again.

When this query is run, on the first row the window frame is just the first row. As the query continues, the frame expands, and unlike subqueries, it doesn't need to refetch any data; it just looks at the data that is already there. Then, when the frame crosses our partition boundary, it resets to just the current row and starts growing again. Instead of hundreds or thousands of trips back and forth to the database to fetch the information, which is what happens with a subquery, the Window Function only needs to make one pass.

This performance difference is so dramatic it can even be seen on the relatively small commissions table. On my laptop, processing the whole 3,000+ rows in the table takes 2.56 seconds to run the self-join version of the query. Contrast that with the Window Function version, which completes instantly. Two and a half seconds isn't much, but as table size increases the speed advantage of Window Functions keeps growing. One of the MariaDB engineers performed some tests on similar, but much larger, tables using a similar query. Table 5-1 shows the results. All times are in seconds.

Table 5-1. *Window Functions Versus Self-joins*

# Rows in Table	Self-join	Self-join with Index	Window Function
10,000	0.29	0.01	0.02
100,000	2.91	0.09	0.16
1,000,000	29.10	2.86	3.04
10,000,000	346.30	90.97	43.17
100,000,000	4357.20	813.20	514.24

Without an index on the table, the Window Function version of the query always wins by an order of magnitude over the self-join version. With an index on the table, the self-join version of the query can keep up with the Window Function version for a while, but after the table gets above a million rows, the Window Function takes the lead and is almost twice as fast.

■ **Note** Window Functions, because of how they operate, don't use indexes at all. They don't even look for them. This can be considered a side benefit to using Window Functions. If you can eliminate expensive self-joins and subqueries by using Window Functions, you may not need to go through the time, effort, and overhead of creating and maintaining indexes.

Ranking Rows in a Result Set

Another common analytical query is to find the top *N* numbers of something, be it the top five selling items, the top ten salaries, or the top three scorers in the youth basketball league.

Using our commissions table again, it is trivial to use SQL to find the top five commissions earned. One way to do it is with the following SQL (with LIMIT 5 to keep the output small):

```
SELECT
  id, salesperson_id AS sid,
  commission_id AS cid,
  commission_amount AS amount,
  commission_date AS date
FROM commissions
ORDER BY commission_amount DESC
LIMIT 5;
```

The result of this query looks like this:

```
+------+-----+-------+--------+------------+
| id   | sid | cid   | amount | date       |
+------+-----+-------+--------+------------+
| 2897 | 121 | 17970 | 499.97 | 2017-11-03 |
| 2269 | 105 | 17340 | 499.90 | 2017-06-15 |
| 1916 | 131 | 16987 | 499.55 | 2017-03-22 |
| 2680 |  66 | 17756 | 499.43 | 2017-09-18 |
| 1610 |  40 | 16688 | 499.41 | 2017-01-16 |
+------+-----+-------+--------+------------+
```

We could improve upon this by doing a JOIN with the employees table to display the name of the employee and their office alongside the commission amount. The following SQL does just that:

```
SELECT
  commissions.commission_date AS date,
  commissions.commission_id AS cid,
  employees.name AS salesperson,
  employees.office AS office,
  commissions.commission_amount AS amount
```

```
FROM commissions LEFT JOIN employees
  ON (commissions.salesperson_id = employees.id)
ORDER BY amount DESC
LIMIT 5;
```

The result looks like the following:

```
+------------+-------+-----------------+-----------+--------+
| date       | cid   | salesperson     | office    | amount |
+------------+-------+-----------------+-----------+--------+
| 2017-11-03 | 17970 | Christina Terry | Wichita   | 499.97 |
| 2017-06-15 | 17340 | Alonzo Page     | Cleveland | 499.90 |
| 2017-03-22 | 16987 | Rene Gibbs      | Dallas    | 499.55 |
| 2017-09-18 | 17756 | Kathryn Barnes  | Dallas    | 499.43 |
| 2017-01-16 | 16688 | Joyce Beck      | Memphis   | 499.41 |
+------------+-------+-----------------+-----------+--------+
```

This is all well and good, and we now know who received the top commissions company-wide, but what if we want to find out the top two commissions from each office? It seems like a reasonable extension of the previous query, but it causes the complexity of our query to jump by quite a bit. There are probably other ways to do this, but here's a query that does it:

```
SELECT * FROM (
  SELECT
    commissions.commission_date AS date,
    commissions.commission_id AS cid,
    employees.name AS salesperson,
    employees.office AS office,
    commissions.commission_amount AS amount
  FROM commissions LEFT JOIN employees
    ON (commissions.salesperson_id = employees.id)
) AS c1
WHERE (
  SELECT count(c2.amount)
  FROM (
    SELECT
      commissions.commission_id AS cid,
      commissions.salesperson_id AS sp_id,
      employees.office AS office,
      commissions.commission_amount AS amount
    FROM commissions LEFT JOIN employees
      ON (commissions.salesperson_id = employees.id)
    ) AS c2
  WHERE
```

```
    c1.cid != c2.cid
    AND
    c1.office = c2.office
    AND
    c2.amount > c1.amount) < 2
ORDER BY office,amount desc;
```

There's a *lot* going on here, but basically we have our original query, some derived tables, and a subquery in our WHERE clause that uses the COUNT function to count the number of commissions in the commissions table that are from the same office AND where the commission amount is greater than the current row, and then limits those results to the top two. That probably stretches the definition of the word *basically* a bit too far. It's quite frankly a bit of a mess, and it's hard for mere humans to read and parse it. On the positive side, it does work. The result of this convoluted query is as follows:

```
+------------+-------+------------------+-------------+--------+
| date       | cid   | salesperson      | office      | amount |
+------------+-------+------------------+-------------+--------+
| 2017-09-22 | 17776 | Jack Green       | Chicago     | 497.83 |
| 2017-05-12 | 17215 | Deborah Peterson | Chicago     | 497.29 |
| 2017-06-15 | 17340 | Alonzo Page      | Cleveland   | 499.90 |
| 2017-05-25 | 17261 | Alonzo Page      | Cleveland   | 499.29 |
| 2017-03-22 | 16987 | Rene Gibbs       | Dallas      | 499.55 |
| 2017-09-18 | 17756 | Kathryn Barnes   | Dallas      | 499.43 |
| 2017-01-16 | 16688 | Joyce Beck       | Memphis     | 499.41 |
| 2017-03-02 | 16890 | Tammy Castro     | Memphis     | 497.58 |
| 2017-12-11 | 18116 | Terrance Reese   | Minneapolis | 499.31 |
| 2017-04-05 | 17047 | Ruby Boyd        | Minneapolis | 495.98 |
| 2017-08-30 | 17674 | Dorothy Anderson | Nauvoo      | 497.91 |
| 2017-12-11 | 18115 | Dorothy Anderson | Nauvoo      | 468.99 |
| 2017-01-20 | 16706 | John Conner      | Raleigh     | 499.33 |
| 2016-08-26 | 16082 | Randal Hogan     | Raleigh     | 499.07 |
| 2017-11-03 | 17970 | Christina Terry  | Wichita     | 499.97 |
| 2016-10-31 | 16345 | Christina Terry  | Wichita     | 497.83 |
+------------+-------+------------------+-------------+--------+
```

Apart from the aforementioned readability issues, the primary downside to this query is that it is slow, especially if there are no indexes on the table. On my laptop, for example, this query takes over ten seconds to run. And even if there were indexes in place, there would be the overhead of creating and maintaining the indexes, which could be problematic if our tables are updated frequently.

A much better and faster way to get at the result we're after is to use Window Functions, specifically the RANK function. To start things off, we can simply take our original query with the JOIN and add the RANK function to it.

Because we want to find out the top two commissions per office, inside the OVER clause we will ORDER BY the commission_amount column from the commissions table and PARTITION BY the office column from the employees table. We'll call the result of the RANK function rnk, to keep things simple.

Lastly, to get the ordering correct, we'll ORDER BY office and our new rnk column. Putting all of that together, we end up with some SQL that looks like the following:

```
SELECT
  RANK() OVER (
    PARTITION BY employees.office
    ORDER BY commissions.commission_amount DESC
  ) AS rnk,
  commissions.commission_date AS date,
  commissions.commission_id AS cid,
  employees.name AS salesperson,
  employees.office AS office,
  commissions.commission_amount AS amount
FROM commissions LEFT JOIN employees
  ON (commissions.salesperson_id = employees.id)
ORDER BY office,rnk;
```

I've removed the LIMIT from this query, so it will output every row in the commissions table, which isn't what we want, but by showing everything we can verify that each row is ranked and partitioned by office correctly. So, we're close.

Here's what the first few rows of the output look like:

```
+-----+------------+-------+------------------+---------+--------+
| rnk | date       | cid   | salesperson      | office  | amount |
+-----+------------+-------+------------------+---------+--------+
|   1 | 2017-09-22 | 17776 | Jack Green       | Chicago | 497.83 |
|   2 | 2017-05-12 | 17215 | Deborah Peterson | Chicago | 497.29 |
|   3 | 2016-11-09 | 16394 | Jack Green       | Chicago | 496.97 |
|   4 | 2016-04-05 | 15486 | Donald Carter    | Chicago | 496.60 |
|   5 | 2017-08-03 | 17566 | Jason Wright     | Chicago | 494.83 |
|   6 | 2016-04-19 | 15549 | Deborah Peterson | Chicago | 494.42 |
|   7 | 2016-10-18 | 16285 | Jack Green       | Chicago | 493.74 |
|   8 | 2017-06-13 | 17324 | Jason Wright     | Chicago | 490.94 |
|   9 | 2016-03-24 | 15441 | Frances Griffin  | Chicago | 488.31 |
|  10 | 2017-10-19 | 17900 | Evelyn Alexander | Chicago | 488.17 |
...
+-----+------------+-------+------------------+---------+--------+
```

Our task now is to limit the output to the top two results from each office. A simple solution would be to add a WHERE rnk <=2 clause that looks for a rank of 2 or less. A quick modification of our query and we get:

```
SELECT
  RANK() OVER (
    PARTITION BY employees.office
    ORDER BY commissions.commission_amount DESC
  ) AS rnk,
  commissions.commission_date AS date,
```

```
  commissions.commission_id AS cid,
  employees.name AS salesperson,
  employees.office AS office,
  commissions.commission_amount AS amount
FROM commissions LEFT JOIN employees
  ON (commissions.salesperson_id = employees.id)
WHERE rnk <= 2
ORDER BY office,rnk;
```

However, when we try to run this new query we get the following error:

```
ERROR 1054 (42S22): Unknown column 'rnk' in 'where clause'
```

On the surface, this error is very confusing. We are referencing the rnk column in both the WHERE and ORDER BY clauses, and they're right next to each other. So, why does it work in the ORDER BY clause and not in the WHERE clause? The reason is the same one we saw before in the ROW_NUMBER example. It bears repeating here: Window Functions aren't computed until after any and all WHERE, HAVING, and GROUP BY clauses are finished. Once they are, the function will run, and only then will the rnk column exist, so with the way our query is written, only the ORDER BY clause can see it.

To solve our problem, we want the WHERE clause to be able to see the rnk column. So, we need to somehow force the RANK function to run prior to our WHERE clause. A simple way to do this is to use a derived table by taking our original query, everything from the initial SELECT down to just before the WHERE clause, and stuff it all into a simple SELECT like so:

```
SELECT * FROM (
<original_query>
) AS ranks
```

For the AS ranks part, we could have used any name, since we don't use or refer to our derived table anywhere else. In this case, the name ranks seemed logical enough.

After adding our derived table wrapper, here's our final query:

```
SELECT * FROM (
  SELECT
    RANK() OVER (
      PARTITION BY employees.office
      ORDER BY commissions.commission_amount DESC
    ) AS rnk,
    commissions.commission_date AS date,
    commissions.commission_id AS cid,
    employees.name AS salesperson,
    employees.office AS office,
    commissions.commission_amount AS amount
  FROM commissions LEFT JOIN employees
    ON (commissions.salesperson_id = employees.id)
) AS ranks
WHERE rnk <= 2
ORDER BY office,rnk;
```

Now that our main query is operating as a derived table, the WHERE clause is able to see the rnk column, and our output is as follows:

rnk	date	cid	salesperson	office	amount
1	2017-09-22	17776	Jack Green	Chicago	497.83
2	2017-05-12	17215	Deborah Peterson	Chicago	497.29
1	2017-06-15	17340	Alonzo Page	Cleveland	499.90
2	2017-05-25	17261	Alonzo Page	Cleveland	499.29
1	2017-03-22	16987	Rene Gibbs	Dallas	499.55
2	2017-09-18	17756	Kathryn Barnes	Dallas	499.43
1	2017-01-16	16688	Joyce Beck	Memphis	499.41
2	2017-03-02	16890	Tammy Castro	Memphis	497.58
1	2017-12-11	18116	Terrance Reese	Minneapolis	499.31
2	2017-04-05	17047	Ruby Boyd	Minneapolis	495.98
1	2017-08-30	17674	Dorothy Anderson	Nauvoo	497.91
2	2017-12-11	18115	Dorothy Anderson	Nauvoo	468.99
1	2017-01-20	16706	John Conner	Raleigh	499.33
2	2016-08-26	16082	Randal Hogan	Raleigh	499.07
1	2017-11-03	17970	Christina Terry	Wichita	499.97
2	2016-10-31	16345	Christina Terry	Wichita	497.83

The only task left now is to try to find out how best to reward these hardworking salespeople. Maybe a gift certificate?

Summary

In this chapter, we explored how *partition_definition*, *order_definition*, and *frame_definition* sections are often used in the OVER clause. We also got to see the ROW_NUMBER and RANK Window Functions in practice, including how to work around some common issues that arise when using them and other Window Functions.

In the next chapter, we'll continue our exploration of Window Functions with a deeper dive into using them to parse and generate graphs of real-world time-series temperature data and analyze fruit sales across a chain of stores.

CHAPTER 6

Window Functions in Practice

This chapter contains several examples that demonstrate using Window Functions in the real world. We'll start with a demonstration of using them multiple times in the same query to see how the WINDOW clause makes this simple and easy to read. Next, we'll explore using Window Functions to help us when we graph time-series data. Lastly, we'll use Window Functions to analyze sales data.

Before We Begin

The examples in this chapter utilize sample data you can use to follow along with the text and experiment with. The first table used in this chapter is called beach, and it can be created with the following query:

```
CREATE TABLE beach (
    day DATE,
    hour TIME,
    temp FLOAT
);
```

The data itself is in a CSV file called bartholomew-ch06-beach.csv and comes from NOAA's Automated Weather Observing System (AWOS). Lots of data is available from them, and it can be accessed from https://www.ncdc.noaa.gov/data-access/land-based-station-data/land-based-datasets/automated-weather-observing-system-awos.

The data can be loaded with a query similar to the following (assuming the file is on the computer running MariaDB server in the /tmp/ folder):

```
LOAD DATA INFILE '/tmp/bartholomew-ch06-beach.csv'
    INTO TABLE beach
    FIELDS TERMINATED BY ','
    OPTIONALLY ENCLOSED BY '"';
```

© Daniel Bartholomew 2017
D. Bartholomew, *MariaDB and MySQL Common Table Expressions and Window Functions Revealed*, https://doi.org/10.1007/978-1-4842-3120-3_6

The second section of this chapter utilizes a table called fruitmart, which can be created with the following query:

```
CREATE TABLE fruitmart (
  store TEXT,
  month DATE,
  fruit TEXT,
  sold  INT
);
```

The data itself is in a CSV file called bartholomew-ch06-fruitmart.csv. It can be loaded with a query similar to the following (assuming the file is on the computer running MariaDB server in the /tmp/ folder):

```
LOAD DATA INFILE '/tmp/bartholomew-ch06-fruitmart.csv'
  INTO TABLE fruitmart
  FIELDS TERMINATED BY ','
  OPTIONALLY ENCLOSED BY '"';
```

■ **Note**   See the "Before We Begin" section of Chapter 1 for extra information about loading the files on Windows and working around issues with secure_file_priv.

We're now ready to begin.

Working with Time-Series Data

The beach table contains temperature records for the year 1984 from Wrightsville Beach in North Carolina, USA. The temperatures are in degrees Celsius.

We can SELECT a sample of this data, say from the first six days of June, to keep the output brief, with the following query:

```
SELECT day, hour, temp
FROM beach
WHERE day BETWEEN '1984-06-01' AND '1984-06-06'
ORDER BY day,hour;
```

Figure 6-1 shows the output.

```
MariaDB 10.2.8
+------------+----------+-------+
| day        | hour     | temp  |
+------------+----------+-------+
| 1984-06-01 | 00:00:00 | 19.4  |
| 1984-06-01 | 06:00:00 | 13.3  |
| 1984-06-01 | 12:00:00 | 12.7  |
| 1984-06-02 | 00:00:00 | 24.9  |
| 1984-06-02 | 18:00:00 | 27.2  |
| 1984-06-03 | 12:00:00 | 21.6  |
| 1984-06-03 | 18:00:00 | 29.4  |
| 1984-06-04 | 06:00:00 | 23.3  |
| 1984-06-04 | 12:00:00 | 23.3  |
| 1984-06-04 | 18:00:00 | 28.8  |
| 1984-06-05 | 00:00:00 | 25.5  |
| 1984-06-05 | 06:00:00 | 22.2  |
| 1984-06-05 | 12:00:00 | 23.3  |
| 1984-06-05 | 18:00:00 | 28.8  |
| 1984-06-06 | 06:00:00 | 23.3  |
| 1984-06-06 | 12:00:00 | 23.3  |
+------------+----------+-------+
16 rows in set (0.01 sec)

MariaDB [ctewf]>
```

Figure 6-1. *Temperatures from June 1–6, 1984*

What's missing from this result is any sort of analysis. We could rely on an external package to take our raw data and do the analysis for us, but Window Functions allow us to do a lot of the analyzing inside the mysql client.

Using Multiple Window Functions at Once

There are several Window Functions that can assist us in analyzing our data as we look for trends. The AVG function can give us the average temperature over a set time period, the MIN function can tell us what the lowest recorded temperature was, and the MAX function can tell us what the maximum temperature was. If we PARTITION BY day to set our frame to each whole day, our output will tell us the information we're looking for, while still showing us all of the individual temperatures (a trick that can't be done easily using regular aggregate functions).

Here's a first attempt at the query:

```
SELECT day, hour, temp,
  AVG(temp) OVER (
    PARTITION BY day
    ORDER BY hour
    ROWS BETWEEN
      UNBOUNDED PRECEDING
      AND
      UNBOUNDED FOLLOWING
  ) AS day_avg,
  MIN(temp) OVER (
    PARTITION BY day
    ORDER BY hour
```

```
    ROWS BETWEEN
      UNBOUNDED PRECEDING
      AND
      UNBOUNDED FOLLOWING
  ) AS day_min,
  MAX(temp) OVER (
    PARTITION BY day
    ORDER BY hour
    ROWS BETWEEN
      UNBOUNDED PRECEDING
      AND
      UNBOUNDED FOLLOWING
  ) AS day_max
FROM beach
WHERE day BETWEEN '1984-06-01' AND '1984-06-06'
ORDER BY day,hour;
```

This query works, but there are some issues, the first of which is the output. We're looking at temperatures, so there's no need for us to have precision on our calculations to 15 decimal points, but that is exactly what each of these functions does by default. Figure 6-2 shows the output.

```
  •  MariaDB 10.2.8
+------------+----------+------+-------------------+---------------------+---------------------+
| day        | hour     | temp | day_avg           | day_min             | day_max             |
+------------+----------+------+-------------------+---------------------+---------------------+
| 1984-06-01 | 00:00:00 | 19.4 | 15.133333206176758 | 12.699999809265137 | 19.399999618530273 |
| 1984-06-01 | 06:00:00 | 13.3 | 15.133333206176758 | 12.699999809265137 | 19.399999618530273 |
| 1984-06-01 | 12:00:00 | 12.7 | 15.133333206176758 | 12.699999809265137 | 19.399999618530273 |
| 1984-06-02 | 00:00:00 | 24.9 | 26.050000190734863 | 24.899999618530273 | 27.200000762939453 |
| 1984-06-02 | 18:00:00 | 27.2 | 26.050000190734863 | 24.899999618530273 | 27.200000762939453 |
| 1984-06-03 | 12:00:00 | 21.6 |              25.5 | 21.600000381469727 | 29.399999618530273 |
| 1984-06-03 | 18:00:00 | 29.4 |              25.5 | 21.600000381469727 | 29.399999618530273 |
| 1984-06-04 | 06:00:00 | 23.3 | 25.13333257039388 | 23.299999237060547 | 28.799999237060547 |
| 1984-06-04 | 12:00:00 | 23.3 | 25.13333257039388 | 23.299999237060547 | 28.799999237060547 |
| 1984-06-04 | 18:00:00 | 28.8 | 25.13333257039388 | 23.299999237060547 | 28.799999237060547 |
| 1984-06-05 | 00:00:00 | 25.5 | 24.949999809265137 | 22.200000762939453 | 28.799999237060547 |
| 1984-06-05 | 06:00:00 | 22.2 | 24.949999809265137 | 22.200000762939453 | 28.799999237060547 |
| 1984-06-05 | 12:00:00 | 23.3 | 24.949999809265137 | 22.200000762939453 | 28.799999237060547 |
| 1984-06-05 | 18:00:00 | 28.8 | 24.949999809265137 | 22.200000762939453 | 28.799999237060547 |
| 1984-06-06 | 06:00:00 | 23.3 | 23.299999237060547 | 23.299999237060547 | 23.299999237060547 |
| 1984-06-06 | 12:00:00 | 23.3 | 23.299999237060547 | 23.299999237060547 | 23.299999237060547 |
+------------+----------+------+-------------------+---------------------+---------------------+
16 rows in set (0.00 sec)

MariaDB [ctewf]>
```

Figure 6-2. *Output with default precision*

Apart from the averages for June 3, the rest of the results are too precise for our needs, so as a first optimization of our query, let's wrap our functions inside the ROUND function, to round to just one decimal of precision, since that matches our original data. Here's our modified query:

```
SELECT day, hour, temp,
  ROUND (AVG(temp) OVER (
    PARTITION BY day
    ORDER BY hour
```

```
    ROWS BETWEEN
      UNBOUNDED PRECEDING
      AND
      UNBOUNDED FOLLOWING
  ),1) AS day_avg,
  ROUND (MIN(temp) OVER (
    PARTITION BY day
    ORDER BY hour
    ROWS BETWEEN
      UNBOUNDED PRECEDING
      AND
      UNBOUNDED FOLLOWING
  ),1) AS day_min,
  ROUND (MAX(temp) OVER (
    PARTITION BY day
    ORDER BY hour
    ROWS BETWEEN
      UNBOUNDED PRECEDING
      AND
      UNBOUNDED FOLLOWING
  ),1) AS day_max
FROM beach
WHERE day BETWEEN '1984-06-01' AND '1984-06-06'
ORDER BY day,hour;
```

Our query is getting a little too complicated for easy parsing by humans, but the output, shown in Figure 6-3, looks much better.

```
•  MariaDB 10.2.8
+------------+----------+-------+---------+---------+---------+
| day        | hour     | temp  | day_avg | day_min | day_max |
+------------+----------+-------+---------+---------+---------+
| 1984-06-01 | 00:00:00 | 19.4  | 15.1    | 12.7    | 19.4    |
| 1984-06-01 | 06:00:00 | 13.3  | 15.1    | 12.7    | 19.4    |
| 1984-06-01 | 12:00:00 | 12.7  | 15.1    | 12.7    | 19.4    |
| 1984-06-02 | 00:00:00 | 24.9  | 26.1    | 24.9    | 27.2    |
| 1984-06-02 | 18:00:00 | 27.2  | 26.1    | 24.9    | 27.2    |
| 1984-06-03 | 12:00:00 | 21.6  | 25.5    | 21.6    | 29.4    |
| 1984-06-03 | 18:00:00 | 29.4  | 25.5    | 21.6    | 29.4    |
| 1984-06-04 | 06:00:00 | 23.3  | 25.1    | 23.3    | 28.8    |
| 1984-06-04 | 12:00:00 | 23.3  | 25.1    | 23.3    | 28.8    |
| 1984-06-04 | 18:00:00 | 28.8  | 25.1    | 23.3    | 28.8    |
| 1984-06-05 | 00:00:00 | 25.5  | 24.9    | 22.2    | 28.8    |
| 1984-06-05 | 06:00:00 | 22.2  | 24.9    | 22.2    | 28.8    |
| 1984-06-05 | 12:00:00 | 23.3  | 24.9    | 22.2    | 28.8    |
| 1984-06-05 | 18:00:00 | 28.8  | 24.9    | 22.2    | 28.8    |
| 1984-06-06 | 06:00:00 | 23.3  | 23.3    | 23.3    | 23.3    |
| 1984-06-06 | 12:00:00 | 23.3  | 23.3    | 23.3    | 23.3    |
+------------+----------+-------+---------+---------+---------+
16 rows in set (0.01 sec)

MariaDB [ctewf]>
```

Figure 6-3. *Rounded results*

Now that we've dealt with the output, it's time to see if we can make the query itself look as nice. Luckily, we have the WINDOW clause to help us clean our query up. This clause was introduced back in Chapter 4, but we haven't used it yet. This is the perfect time to do so. All of our OVER clauses are identical, so we can create one WINDOW clause and have all of the OVER clauses just refer to it, like so:

```
SELECT day, hour, temp,
  ROUND (AVG(temp) OVER w1,1) AS day_avg,
  ROUND (MIN(temp) OVER w1,1) AS day_min,
  ROUND (MAX(temp) OVER w1,1) AS day_max
FROM beach
WHERE day BETWEEN '1984-06-01' AND '1984-06-06'
WINDOW
  w1 AS (
    PARTITION BY day
    ORDER BY day,hour
    ROWS BETWEEN
      UNBOUNDED PRECEDING
      AND
      UNBOUNDED FOLLOWING
  )
ORDER BY day,hour;
```

With the WINDOW clause in place the query is instantly more understandable. It is especially easy now to see how the ROUND function wraps around our Window Functions. And the output is the same. Win-win!

A side benefit of making the query more readable is that it becomes easier to extend it by adding a second window definition to our WINDOW clause. For example, we can define additional columns that give the min, max, and average temperatures over our entire result set, like so:

```
SELECT day, hour, temp,
  ROUND (AVG(temp) OVER w1,1) AS day_avg,
  ROUND (MIN(temp) OVER w1,1) AS day_min,
  ROUND (MAX(temp) OVER w1,1) AS day_max,
  ROUND (AVG(temp) OVER w2,1) AS all_avg,
  ROUND (MAX(temp) OVER w2,1) AS all_max,
  ROUND (MIN(temp) OVER w2,1) AS all_min
FROM beach
WHERE day BETWEEN '1984-06-01' AND '1984-06-06'
WINDOW
  w1 AS (
    PARTITION BY day
    ORDER BY day,hour
    ROWS BETWEEN
      UNBOUNDED PRECEDING
      AND
      UNBOUNDED FOLLOWING
```

```
),
w2 AS (
  ORDER BY day,hour
  ROWS BETWEEN
    UNBOUNDED PRECEDING
    AND
    UNBOUNDED FOLLOWING
)
ORDER BY day,hour;
```

Keeping in mind that our result set is only six days, and that a month would be more meaningful, the result is shown in Figure 6-4.

```
● MariaDB 10.2.8
+------------+----------+-------+---------+---------+---------+---------+---------+---------+
| day        | hour     | temp  | day_avg | day_min | day_max | all_avg | all_max | all_min |
+------------+----------+-------+---------+---------+---------+---------+---------+---------+
| 1984-06-01 | 00:00:00 | 19.4  | 15.1    | 12.7    | 19.4    | 23.1    | 29.4    | 12.7    |
| 1984-06-01 | 06:00:00 | 13.3  | 15.1    | 12.7    | 19.4    | 23.1    | 29.4    | 12.7    |
| 1984-06-01 | 12:00:00 | 12.7  | 15.1    | 12.7    | 19.4    | 23.1    | 29.4    | 12.7    |
| 1984-06-02 | 00:00:00 | 24.9  | 26.1    | 24.9    | 27.2    | 23.1    | 29.4    | 12.7    |
| 1984-06-02 | 18:00:00 | 27.2  | 26.1    | 24.9    | 27.2    | 23.1    | 29.4    | 12.7    |
| 1984-06-03 | 12:00:00 | 21.6  | 25.5    | 21.6    | 29.4    | 23.1    | 29.4    | 12.7    |
| 1984-06-03 | 18:00:00 | 29.4  | 25.5    | 21.6    | 29.4    | 23.1    | 29.4    | 12.7    |
| 1984-06-04 | 06:00:00 | 23.3  | 25.1    | 23.3    | 28.8    | 23.1    | 29.4    | 12.7    |
| 1984-06-04 | 12:00:00 | 23.3  | 25.1    | 23.3    | 28.8    | 23.1    | 29.4    | 12.7    |
| 1984-06-04 | 18:00:00 | 28.8  | 25.1    | 23.3    | 28.8    | 23.1    | 29.4    | 12.7    |
| 1984-06-05 | 00:00:00 | 25.5  | 24.9    | 22.2    | 28.8    | 23.1    | 29.4    | 12.7    |
| 1984-06-05 | 06:00:00 | 22.2  | 24.9    | 22.2    | 28.8    | 23.1    | 29.4    | 12.7    |
| 1984-06-05 | 12:00:00 | 23.3  | 24.9    | 22.2    | 28.8    | 23.1    | 29.4    | 12.7    |
| 1984-06-05 | 18:00:00 | 28.8  | 24.9    | 22.2    | 28.8    | 23.1    | 29.4    | 12.7    |
| 1984-06-06 | 06:00:00 | 23.3  | 23.3    | 23.3    | 23.3    | 23.1    | 29.4    | 12.7    |
| 1984-06-06 | 12:00:00 | 23.3  | 23.3    | 23.3    | 23.3    | 23.1    | 29.4    | 12.7    |
+------------+----------+-------+---------+---------+---------+---------+---------+---------+
16 rows in set (0.00 sec)

MariaDB [ctewf]>
```

Figure 6-4. Adding additional columns to the output

It would be nice if we could optimize our query to get rid of the duplicated <frame_ definition> sections in our w1 and w2 WINDOW definitions, but the syntax rules of ordering in WINDOW definitions make this impossible.

Graphing Time-Series Results

The analysis that we've done so far is pretty good, but we're still just looking at numbers. This makes it hard to visualize trends over time. Maybe not so much when we're just looking at six days, but if we expand our query to cover a whole month, all the numbers start to blur together, at least they do for me. A graph is a good way to condense a large amount of data into something that can be understood at a glance. The mysql command-line client program doesn't have any graphing capabilities of its own, but there are many external tools that can help us do this. One popular tool is called *gnuplot*. It is readily available on Linux from your distribution's package repository, or for those on Windows it can be downloaded from the main gnuplot website at http://gnuplot.info/.

Before running the following examples, test your gnuplot installation to ensure it is working properly. Refer to the gnuplot documentation for help, if needed.

The gnuplot program expects data to be in columns separated by whitespace (tabs and/or spaces). To export our data to a file that gnuplot can read, we could simply add the following line to any of our previous queries before the semicolon (;):

```
INTO OUTFILE '/tmp/out.dat'
```

However, there are some downsides to this. One is if the secure_file_priv option is enabled on your MariaDB or MySQL server, in which case you're limited to writing files to the directory configured. If you add the preceding line to a query and get the following error, you're affected:

```
ERROR 1290 (HY000): The MySQL server is running with the --secure-file-priv
option so it cannot execute this statement
```

In such a case you can either disable the option in your my.cnf or my.ini file and restart your MySQL or MariaDB server, or direct your output to the configured directory. You can see what directory is configured with the following command:

```
SHOW VARIABLES LIKE 'secure_file_priv';
```

Another issue with using INTO OUTFILE is that MySQL or MariaDB will refuse to overwrite a file if it already exists. This is a safety measure, but it can be annoying to deal with when you just want to quickly rerun a query after tweaking it a little.

A way around both of these limitations, and one which is especially helpful when querying a database on an automated basis, is to call the mysql command-line client from the shell, wrapping the query like this:

```
mysql -p --column-names=0 <database_name> -e "<query>" > /tmp/out.dat
```

Replace *<database_name>* with the name of the database the table is in, and replace *<query>* with the actual query. In this example, we're exporting our data to the file /tmp/out.dat, but we could put it anywhere that is convenient on our server. It also has the benefit, and also the danger, that every time it is run, the file we're outputting to is overwritten with the new result.

If you're not familiar with it, the --column-names=0 flag removes the column headings from the output. We don't need them, and they will confuse gnuplot if they're included.

Let's plot the data from our beach table. Here is a simple query that outputs all of the temperatures from every day in our beach table:

```
SELECT day, hour, temp
FROM beach
ORDER BY day,hour
INTO OUTFILE '/tmp/out.dat';
```

And here's the same query as it might be run from the shell using the mysql command-line client. It assumes the database, where all of the sample tables are, is named apress:

```
mysql -p --column-names=0 apress -e "
  SELECT day, hour, temp
  FROM beach
  ORDER BY day,hour;
" > /tmp/out.dat
```

To keep the queries consistent, for the rest of this section we'll use this variant of the query in our examples.

Whichever method we use to get the results of our query into a file, we are now ready to plot our data using gnuplot. After being started from the command-line shell, gnuplot will show a gnuplot> prompt and will be ready to accept commands. We can enter the following commands to create a graph:

```
set xdata time
set style data lines
set timefmt "%Y-%m-%d   %H:%m:%s"
set format x "%b"
set xlabel "1984 Wrightsville Beach Temperatures"
set ylabel "Temperature in Degrees C"
set autoscale y
set xrange ["1984-01-01":"1984-12-31"]
plot "/tmp/out.dat" using 1:3 title "Temperature" with lines
```

Some of these commands, like xlabel and ylabel, which set the labels for the x- and y-axes, are self-explanatory, others not so much. Documentation is built into gnuplot, so if you are wondering about what any of the commands do, you can look them up. For example, the following will show you the documentation for the set xrange command:

```
help set xrange
```

After the plot command, gnuplot will open a window with a graph of the data. It should look similar to Figure 6-5.

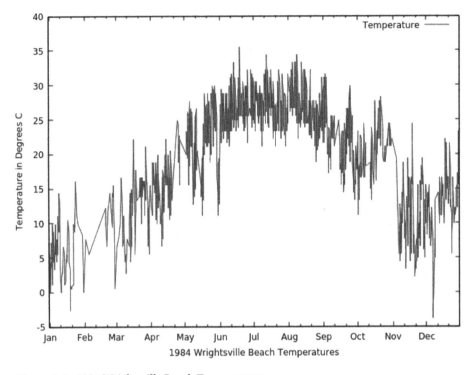

Figure 6-5. *1984 Wrightsville Beach Temperatures*

■ **Note**   If we are running gnuplot on a remote server, we will need to tell it to export our graph directly to a file. To do this, we can add the following two lines to our gnuplot commands, before the plot line:

```
set terminal png size 640,480 enhanced
```

```
set output 'output.png'
```

With these two lines entered, after we run the plot line our graph will be output to a file called output.png in our current working directory.

An alternative on Linux is to ssh to the remote database server with X11 forwarding enabled using the -X flag, e.g., with ssh -X <remote_host>. This way, when running the plot command, gnuplot will open the graph in a window.

Looking at the graph, there are a few interesting things to see. One is how in February and October we're missing some data, causing gaps in the graph. It is also easy to see how temperatures from morning to evening vary, sometimes by quite a bit. However, with all of the up and down movement of the lines, it's hard to get a sense of the average temperature at Wrightsville Beach over the course of the year. This is easy to do by using the AVG Window Function to generate a smoother line. We can modify the original query to include a new column, average, that looks at the current row, the previous ten rows, and the following ten rows. The effect of this will smooth things out, like so:

```
mysql -p --column-names=0 apress -e "
SELECT day, hour, temp,
  AVG(temp) over (
    ORDER BY day,hour
    ROWS BETWEEN
      10 PRECEDING
      AND
      10 FOLLOWING
) AS average
FROM beach
ORDER BY day,hour;
" > /tmp/out.dat
```

We can then launch gnuplot and run the following commands to generate our new plot:

```
set xdata time
set style data lines
set timefmt "%Y-%m-%d   %H:%m:%s"
set format x "%b"
set xlabel "1984 Wrightsville Beach Temperatures"
set ylabel "Temperature in Degrees C"
set autoscale y
set linetype 2 linewidth 4
set xrange ["1984-01-01":"1984-12-31"]
plot "/tmp/out.dat" using 1:3 title "Temperature" with lines, \
    "/tmp/out.dat" using 1:4 title "Average" with lines
```

These commands are mostly identical to the previous gnuplot commands, with a couple of key additions. First, the plot command (now split over two lines to make it more readable) has an additional data line defined, the average column from our output. And second, there is a set linetype command that makes the line on the graph that shows the *Average* as thicker than the *Temperature* line to make it stand out better. The gnuplot output should look similar to Figure 6-6.

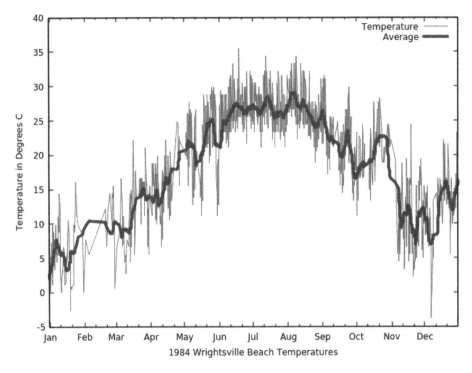

Figure 6-6. *1984 Wrightsville Beach Temperatures, with average*

If the average line is still too rough, we can just change the tens in our query to higher numbers and then rerun the gnuplot commands.

Being able to efficiently analyze time-series data like this is becoming more important with the rise of the Internet of Things. More and more sensors, all collecting their various bits of data, surround us every day. Aggregate Window Functions like AVG provide new tools to help analyze and work with this data.

Analyzing Fruit Sales

The rest of this chapter will focus on an imaginary fruit company named FruitMart. The company has ten stores scattered around North Carolina, USA, and they sell five different kinds of fruit. Our task is to analyze the sales data so we can effectively run the business.

Fruit Sales Within a Single Store

One very useful bit of analysis to perform is to compare how fruit sales change from month to month. The LEAD and LAG functions let us compare a value to the next and previous months' sales directly.

Learning from previous examples, we'll define a WINDOW clause that contains our PARTITION BY and ORDER BY clauses. For this example, we're only interested in comparing sales in a given store to sales in the same store, so we'll PARTITION BY store. We'll also add fruit to the partition so that we don't compare apples to oranges (sorry, I couldn't resist).

Next, we'll ORDER BY both store and month to keep our output sane. In our final ORDER BY clause we'll switch this up and ORDER BY fruit,store. This has the effect of showing us all of the apples results for all stores, then all of the bananas, and so on.

Unfortunately, the complete output is quite large, so to keep the output brief we'll add a WHERE clause that restricts our query to a single store, Durham, and a single fruit, oranges.

Here's our completed query:

```
SELECT store, month, fruit, sold,
  LAG(sold)  OVER w1 AS prev,
  LEAD(sold) OVER w1 AS next
FROM fruitmart
WHERE fruit = 'oranges'
  AND store = 'Durham'
WINDOW w1 AS (
  PARTITION BY fruit,store
  ORDER BY store,month
)
ORDER BY fruit,store;
```

Figure 6-7 shows the output.

```
•  MariaDB 10.2.8
+--------+------------+---------+------+------+------+
| store  | month      | fruit   | sold | prev | next |
+--------+------------+---------+------+------+------+
| Durham | 2016-01-01 | oranges |  244 | NULL |   29 |
| Durham | 2016-02-01 | oranges |   29 |  244 |  153 |
| Durham | 2016-03-01 | oranges |  153 |   29 |  297 |
| Durham | 2016-04-01 | oranges |  297 |  153 |   16 |
| Durham | 2016-05-01 | oranges |   16 |  297 |  930 |
| Durham | 2016-06-01 | oranges |  930 |   16 |  320 |
| Durham | 2016-07-01 | oranges |  320 |  930 |  393 |
| Durham | 2016-08-01 | oranges |  393 |  320 |  292 |
| Durham | 2016-09-01 | oranges |  292 |  393 |  396 |
| Durham | 2016-10-01 | oranges |  396 |  292 |  379 |
| Durham | 2016-11-01 | oranges |  379 |  396 |  432 |
| Durham | 2016-12-01 | oranges |  432 |  379 | NULL |
+--------+------------+---------+------+------+------+
12 rows in set (0.02 sec)

MariaDB [ctewf]> ▌
```

Figure 6-7. *Oranges sold from the Durham store*

The first prev column is NULL because there are no previous entries for the LAG function to view. The same is true for the last next column, where there are no additional entries for the LEAD column.

If we want to view the complete results for all stores, we just need to remove the following two lines from the query and rerun it:

```
WHERE fruit = 'oranges'
  AND store = 'Durham'
```

Viewing our results chronologically like this is useful, but you may wonder what the point is; after all, the prev and next values can be easily seen by just looking at the previous and next rows.

Having them on one line comes in handy when ranking sales. We can add the RANK function to our query and then sort by the rank in our final ORDER BY clause. It needs a slightly different OVER clause, so we won't use the w1 WINDOW the other two Window Functions use. Instead, we'll define a w2 WINDOW to use with it.

While we're at it, we can extend the new w2 WINDOW to create a w3 WINDOW we can use to get the average sales for a given fruit at a given store.

Here's the full query:

```
SELECT store, month, fruit, sold,
  LAG(sold)       OVER w1  AS prev,
  LEAD(sold)      OVER w1  AS next,
  ROUND(AVG(sold) OVER w3) AS avg,
  RANK()          OVER w2  AS rnk
FROM fruitmart
WHERE fruit = 'oranges'
  AND store = 'Durham'
WINDOW
  w1 AS (
    PARTITION BY fruit,store
    ORDER BY store,month
  ),
  w2 AS (
    PARTITION BY fruit,store
    ORDER BY sold DESC
  ),
  w3 AS (w2
    ROWS BETWEEN
      UNBOUNDED PRECEDING
      AND
      UNBOUNDED FOLLOWING
  )
ORDER BY fruit,store,rnk;
```

The results, shown in Figure 6-8, are obviously more interesting than before.

```
●  MariaDB 10.2.8                                                                     ●●●
+--------+------------+---------+------+------+------+-----+-----+
| store  | month      | fruit   | sold | prev | next | avg | rnk |
+--------+------------+---------+------+------+------+-----+-----+
| Durham | 2016-06-01 | oranges |  930 |   16 |  320 | 323 |   1 |
| Durham | 2016-12-01 | oranges |  432 |  379 | NULL | 323 |   2 |
| Durham | 2016-10-01 | oranges |  396 |  292 |  379 | 323 |   3 |
| Durham | 2016-08-01 | oranges |  393 |  320 |  292 | 323 |   4 |
| Durham | 2016-11-01 | oranges |  379 |  396 |  432 | 323 |   5 |
| Durham | 2016-07-01 | oranges |  320 |  930 |  393 | 323 |   6 |
| Durham | 2016-04-01 | oranges |  297 |  153 |   16 | 323 |   7 |
| Durham | 2016-09-01 | oranges |  292 |  393 |  396 | 323 |   8 |
| Durham | 2016-01-01 | oranges |  244 | NULL |   29 | 323 |   9 |
| Durham | 2016-03-01 | oranges |  153 |   29 |  297 | 323 |  10 |
| Durham | 2016-02-01 | oranges |   29 |  244 |  153 | 323 |  11 |
| Durham | 2016-05-01 | oranges |   16 |  297 |  930 | 323 |  12 |
+--------+------------+---------+------+------+------+-----+-----+
12 rows in set (0.00 sec)

MariaDB [ctewf]>
```

Figure 6-8. Oranges sold from the Durham store with averages and ranks

For starters, our highest sales were 930 in June, but thanks to the prev and next columns we can see that it wasn't really part of a broader trend; in fact, in the previous month we had our lowest sales of the year for oranges in Durham, 16, and in the following month we dropped down almost exactly to our average number of sales, 323.

It might also be worth investigating why our three lowest months were all preceded by lower-than-average months.

As with the previous query, we can remove the WHERE clause to look at the results for all fruit sales at all of our stores, or simply modify it to select a different store and/or fruit.

Comparing Fruit Sales Across All Stores

Analyzing a single store's sales performance is good, but it would also be useful to do additional analysis comparing all our stores.

The changes needed to alter our query to compare fruit sales from all stores are actually quite minimal.

First, we need to have the rnk column apply across a given fruit for all stores. This can be done by simply removing store from the PARTITION BY clause in the w2 WINDOW.

With the change to w2 in place, our avg column will now compute the average for all sales of a given fruit. But it might be useful to still list the store sales average. For that we will define a new WINDOW, w4, which re-creates what the w2 + w3 combination used to be. We'll call this new column s_avg for store average, and for good measure we should change the avg column to a_avg for all average.

The last change is to remove store from the final ORDER BY clause. This is just to get the rankings to line up properly.

Here's the query:

```
SELECT store, month, fruit, sold,
  LAG(sold)      OVER w1  AS prev,
  LEAD(sold)     OVER w1  AS next,
```

```
    ROUND(AVG(sold) OVER w4) AS s_avg,
    ROUND(AVG(sold) OVER w3) AS a_avg,
    RANK()          OVER w2  AS rnk
FROM fruitmart
WHERE fruit = 'oranges'
WINDOW
  w1 AS (
    PARTITION BY fruit,store
    ORDER BY store,month
  ),
  w2 AS (
    PARTITION BY fruit
    ORDER BY sold DESC
  ),
  w3 AS (w2
    ROWS BETWEEN
      UNBOUNDED PRECEDING
      AND
      UNBOUNDED FOLLOWING
  ),
  w4 AS (
    PARTITION BY fruit,store
    ORDER BY sold DESC
    ROWS BETWEEN
      UNBOUNDED PRECEDING
      AND
      UNBOUNDED FOLLOWING
  )
ORDER BY fruit,rnk;
```

As before, the WHERE clause can be removed to show all fruits. It's just in our query to lessen the amount of output. Of course, now that we're looking at oranges across all stores, there's ten times more output than before, but Figure 6-9 shows the first five and last five rows of the result.

store	month	fruit	sold	prev	next	s_avg	a_avg	rnk
Greensboro	2016-04-01	oranges	998	613	4	443	498	1
Hickory	2016-04-01	oranges	968	749	452	661	498	2
Gastonia	2016-09-01	oranges	967	32	226	376	498	3
Kinston	2016-05-01	oranges	967	100	789	562	498	3
Kinston	2016-12-01	oranges	949	206	NULL	562	498	5
...								
Raleigh	2016-10-01	oranges	31	296	889	434	498	116
Durham	2016-02-01	oranges	29	244	153	323	498	117
Gastonia	2016-05-01	oranges	20	891	68	376	498	118
Durham	2016-05-01	oranges	16	297	930	323	498	119
Greensboro	2016-05-01	oranges	4	998	359	443	498	120

```
120 rows in set (0.00 sec)

MariaDB [ctewf]>
```

Figure 6-9. *Orange sales from all stores*

One very odd but potentially useful thing from our results is that the bottom three sales months are all from May. But May was also when Kinston had its highest sales of the year. How did this happen? Were there shipping issues? Something in Kinston that pulled oranges away from the other stores? Something else? Definitely something to investigate.

Summary

In this chapter, we explored some examples of using Window Functions in the real world. We used multiple Window Functions in a single query, plotted results for when we are dealing with lots of data, and then used Window Functions to analyze sales in various ways at a fictional fruit company. For the next chapter, we'll tie the first and second half of the book together by using both CTEs and Window Functions together.

CHAPTER 7

Combining Window Functions and CTEs

Window Functions and CTEs are great in isolation, but they can also be very useful together. This chapter will walk through some examples that demonstrate how Window Functions and CTEs can be used together. We'll start with a simple averaging of rainfall data, then move on to how to use CTEs and Window Functions together to fix a common schema issue. Lastly, we'll use them to do some deeper analysis on our rainfall data to find gaps and islands in our data set.

Before We Begin

The table used for the examples in this chapter is called precip and can be created with the following query:

```
CREATE TABLE precip (
  location TEXT,
  day DATE,
  precip FLOAT
);
```

The data is in a CSV file called bartholomew-ch07-precip.csv. It can be loaded with a query similar to the following (assuming the file is on the computer running MariaDB or MySQL server in the /tmp/ folder):

```
LOAD DATA INFILE '/tmp/bartholomew-ch07-precip.csv'
  INTO TABLE precip
  FIELDS TERMINATED BY ','
  OPTIONALLY ENCLOSED BY '"';
```

Note   See the "Before We Begin" section of Chapter 1 for extra information about loading the files on Windows and working around issues with secure_file_priv.

© Daniel Bartholomew 2017
D. Bartholomew, *MariaDB and MySQL Common Table Expressions and Window Functions Revealed*, https://doi.org/10.1007/978-1-4842-3120-3_7

We're now ready to begin.

Compute the Average Time Between Days with Precipitation

The precip table contains data on when it rained, and how much, for the year 1976 for three cities in North Carolina, USA: Asheville, Raleigh, and Wilmington. The data comes from the National Oceanic and Atmospheric Administration (NOAA) website at https://www.ncdc.noaa.gov/cdo-web/search.

One common query when analyzing precipitation or other time-based data is to compute what the average time is between events, which for our data means the average number of days between when it rains.

By using a CTE without a Window Function we can, in a slightly convoluted way, select from the precip table, and then as we walk through our results we use the DATEDIFF function to determine the number of days between the current date and the largest previous date we looked at, using a self-join to ensure that we're looking at the correct data.

Our completed *<cte_body>* section looks like this:

```
SELECT
  p1.location,
  p1.day, MAX(p2.day),
  DATEDIFF(p1.day, MAX(p2.day)) AS diff
FROM precip AS p1,
     precip AS p2
WHERE
  p1.location = p2.location
  AND
  p2.day < p1.day
GROUP BY p1.day,p1.location
ORDER BY location;
```

The first ten rows of the output of this query look like this:

```
+------------+------------+-------------+------+
| location   | day        | MAX(p2.day) | diff |
+------------+------------+-------------+------+
| Asheville  | 1976-01-07 | 1976-01-03  |    4 |
| Asheville  | 1976-01-13 | 1976-01-07  |    6 |
| Asheville  | 1976-01-16 | 1976-01-13  |    3 |
| Asheville  | 1976-01-17 | 1976-01-16  |    1 |
| Asheville  | 1976-01-26 | 1976-01-17  |    9 |
| Asheville  | 1976-01-27 | 1976-01-26  |    1 |
| Asheville  | 1976-02-01 | 1976-01-27  |    5 |
| Asheville  | 1976-02-02 | 1976-02-01  |    1 |
| Asheville  | 1976-02-15 | 1976-02-02  |   13 |
| Asheville  | 1976-02-18 | 1976-02-15  |    3 |
...
+------------+------------+-------------+------+
```

For our *<cte_query>* section, we want to GROUP BY our location column and use the AVG function to compute the average of the diff column. Calling our CTE precip_avg, here is our completed query:

```
WITH precip_avg AS (
  SELECT
    p1.location,
    p1.day, MAX(p2.day),
    DATEDIFF(p1.day, MAX(p2.day)) AS diff
  FROM precip AS p1,
       precip AS p2
  WHERE
    p1.location = p2.location
    AND
    p2.day < p1.day
  GROUP BY p1.day,p1.location
  ORDER BY location
)
SELECT
  location,
  AVG(diff) AS avg_days
FROM precip_avg
GROUP BY location
ORDER BY location;
```

The results are:

```
+------------+----------+
| location   | avg_days |
+------------+----------+
| Asheville  | 3.3611   |
| Raleigh    | 3.7423   |
| Wilmington | 3.3645   |
+------------+----------+
```

This query is good, but we can simplify it by using the LAG Window Function to eliminate the need to do a self-join.

As before, we'll start with the *<cte_body>* section, where instead of the self-join we just call the LAG function with the day column as the value, partitioning by location and ordering by the day column. This query looks like this:

```
SELECT
  location,day,
  LAG(day) OVER (
    PARTITION BY location
    ORDER BY day
  ) AS prev_day
FROM precip;
```

The output of this query is different than what we got from our self-join version:

```
+------------+------------+------------+
| location   | day        | prev_day   |
+------------+------------+------------+
| Asheville  | 1976-01-03 | NULL       |
| Asheville  | 1976-01-07 | 1976-01-03 |
| Asheville  | 1976-01-13 | 1976-01-07 |
| Asheville  | 1976-01-16 | 1976-01-13 |
| Asheville  | 1976-01-17 | 1976-01-16 |
| Asheville  | 1976-01-26 | 1976-01-17 |
| Asheville  | 1976-01-27 | 1976-01-26 |
| Asheville  | 1976-02-01 | 1976-01-27 |
| Asheville  | 1976-02-02 | 1976-02-01 |
| Asheville  | 1976-02-15 | 1976-02-02 |
...
+------------+------------+------------+
```

The main difference is the addition of the first row with the NULL result for the prev_ day column. The other main difference is that we don't have a diff column, because we removed the DATEDIFF function.

Because the output is different, we need to change the *<cte_query>* section a bit. We'll start by adding back the DATEDIFF function, this time inside of the AVG function, and because it is now outside of the *<cte_body>* we can simply call it with the day column and the new prev_day column generated by the LAG function.

Our much simpler query now looks like this:

```
WITH precip_avg AS (
  SELECT
    location,day,
    LAG(day) OVER (
      PARTITION BY location
      ORDER BY day
    ) AS prev_day
  FROM precip
)
SELECT location,
  AVG(DATEDIFF(day, prev_day)) AS avg_day
FROM precip_avg
GROUP BY location;
```

Our query has only gone from 19 lines to 13, but the readability is much better without the confusing self-join in place. More importantly, the result is the same, and a by-product of removing the self-join is a nice performance boost. Or at least we would see a performance boost if our table were larger; our data set is simply too small to see much of a difference.

Adding a Primary Key Column

Not all tables are perfect. Some would say that no tables are ever truly perfect. It's a fact of life that tables are modified periodically due to updated requirements, maintenance, errors, and a host of other reasons.

Let's say a request comes in while you're away on vacation to add a `precip_id` column to the `precip` table, but instead of adding the column as an auto-incrementing primary key, a junior DBA adds it as an `INT` with a default value assigned as hexadecimal number 1a for some unknown reason. Here's the code the junior DBA ran that does this:

```
ALTER TABLE precip
  ADD COLUMN precip_id INT DEFAULT 0x1a FIRST;
```

Because this is a new column, when the `ALTER TABLE` goes through, the `precip_id` column gets assigned the value *26*, the decimal equivalent of hexadecimal *1a*, on every row. Sometime later, you discover this error, and your task is to now fix the mess and `ALTER` the `precip` table so that the `precip_id` column is an auto-incrementing primary key, like it was originally supposed to be.

We could try to do the following:

```
ALTER TABLE precip
  MODIFY COLUMN precip_id SERIAL PRIMARY KEY FIRST;
```

But because the `service_id` columns for every row already have values in them, we'll get the following error instead of what we want:

```
ERROR 1062 (23000): ALTER TABLE causes auto_increment resequencing,
resulting in duplicate entry '26' for key 'PRIMARY'
```

Another option would be to drop or rename the current `precip_id` column and then add it back with the correct definition. For the sake of this example, let's assume this solution is not an option.

So, what do we do? Thanks to Window Functions and Common Table Expressions, there is a third option we can use. The idea is to combine a Common Table Expression with the `ROW_NUMBER` Window Function to produce a table that looks like how we want the `precip` table to end up. We then use this CTE-derived table as the source for updating the actual `precip` table.

Unfortunately, this trick only works on MySQL right now, but the MariaDB developers will probably add support for it before too long.

We start by defining our *<cte_body>*. This will be a simple `SELECT` statement, ordered by the `service_date` column, with the `ROW_NUMBER` Window Function there to give each row of output a unique number. The code looks like this:

```
SELECT
  ROW_NUMBER() OVER(
    ORDER BY day
  ) AS rnum,
```

```
  location, day, precip
FROM precip
ORDER BY day;
```

The first few rows of output for this query, when run by itself, look like the following:

```
+------+------------+------------+--------+
| rnum | location   | day        | precip |
+------+------------+------------+--------+
|    1 | Asheville  | 1976-01-03 |    0.2 |
|    2 | Wilmington | 1976-01-03 |   0.01 |
|    3 | Raleigh    | 1976-01-03 |   0.09 |
|    4 | Wilmington | 1976-01-04 |   0.11 |
|    5 | Asheville  | 1976-01-07 |   0.36 |
|    6 | Wilmington | 1976-01-07 |   0.07 |
|    7 | Raleigh    | 1976-01-07 |   0.47 |
|    8 | Wilmington | 1976-01-08 |   0.16 |
|    9 | Raleigh    | 1976-01-08 |    0.1 |
|   10 | Wilmington | 1976-01-11 |   0.01 |
...
+------+------------+------------+--------+
```

For a *<cte_name>*, let's use precip_update, so we'll wrap our *<cte_body>* with a WITH precip_update AS clause.

We now come to the *<cte_query>* section. Instead of a SELECT statement like we've used with previous CTE examples, this time we'll use an UPDATE statement. In this statement, we first need to refer both our CTE and our original precip table. Then, we SET the precip.precip_id to the value of precip_update.rnum wherever both the location and day match between these two tables.

The final code looks like this:

```
WITH precip_update AS (
  SELECT
    ROW_NUMBER() OVER(
      ORDER BY day
    ) AS rnum,
    location, day, precip
  FROM precip
  ORDER BY day
)
UPDATE precip, precip_update
  SET precip.precip_id = precip_update.rnum
  WHERE
    precip.location = precip_update.location
    AND
    precip.day = precip_update.day;
```

As is usual with UPDATE commands, the output will simply tell us how many rows were matched and changed and if there were any warnings.

■ **Note**   If you try running this query using a graphical client, such as MySQL Workbench, you may get an error about *safe update mode* being enabled. If that happens, either switch to using the command-line mysql client or disable safe mode in *Preferences > SQL* Editor and reconnect.

To view the change, we can issue a simple SELECT:

```
SELECT * FROM precip ORDER BY precip_id;
```

The first few rows of output look like this:

```
+-----------+-------------+------------+--------+
| precip_id | location    | day        | precip |
+-----------+-------------+------------+--------+
|         1 | Asheville   | 1976-01-03 |    0.2 |
|         2 | Wilmington  | 1976-01-03 |   0.01 |
|         3 | Raleigh     | 1976-01-03 |   0.09 |
|         4 | Wilmington  | 1976-01-04 |   0.11 |
|         5 | Asheville   | 1976-01-07 |   0.36 |
|         6 | Wilmington  | 1976-01-07 |   0.07 |
|         7 | Raleigh     | 1976-01-07 |   0.47 |
|         8 | Wilmington  | 1976-01-08 |   0.16 |
|         9 | Raleigh     | 1976-01-08 |    0.1 |
|        10 | Wilmington  | 1976-01-11 |   0.01 |
...
+-----------+-------------+------------+--------+
```

We're not done at this point, but the final step is pretty simple. If we DESCRIBE precip, we'll see that our precip_id column is still not a primary key, nor does it auto-increment:

```
+-----------+---------+------+-----+---------+-------+
| Field     | Type    | Null | Key | Default | Extra |
+-----------+---------+------+-----+---------+-------+
| precip_id | int(11) | YES  |     | 26      |       |
| location  | text    | YES  |     | NULL    |       |
| day       | date    | YES  |     | NULL    |       |
| precip    | float   | YES  |     | NULL    |       |
+-----------+---------+------+-----+---------+-------+
```

However, now that every row of our `precip_id` column is a unique number, thanks to the ROW_NUMBER Window Function, we can issue the ALTER TABLE command that failed before:

```
ALTER TABLE precip MODIFY COLUMN precip_id SERIAL PRIMARY KEY FIRST;
```

This time, ALTER TABLE succeeds, and if we DESCRIBE precip, again, we'll see that our `precip_id` column is exactly what we want:

```
+-----------+---------------------+------+-----+---------+----------------+
| Field     | Type                | Null | Key | Default | Extra          |
+-----------+---------------------+------+-----+---------+----------------+
| precip_id | bigint(20) unsigned | NO   | PRI | NULL    | auto_increment |
| location  | text                | YES  |     | NULL    |                |
| day       | date                | YES  |     | NULL    |                |
| precip    | float               | YES  |     | NULL    |                |
+-----------+---------------------+------+-----+---------+----------------+
```

Finding Gaps and Islands

Serialized and time-based data generally arrives at a pre-determined time, such as every time a polling process kicks off. But sometimes there are unexpected gaps in the data, or like in the case of weather data such as in our `precip` table, gaps are expected. It doesn't rain every day, after all.

When analyzing such data, finding these gaps and islands of data can be very useful.

Gaps

To find gaps in our data, we basically have to look at times when our expected interval is skipped. In the case of our `precip` table, the expected interval is one day. Every day, if there was precipitation, a row was added to the table.

The LEAD Window Function is perfect for looking at a given row and finding out what the next row is, so it makes sense to include that function in our <cte_body>. Other elements we should include are a column with the current day we are on, using the DAYOFYEAR function to make the math simpler. We'll need the same thing with the column we use to hold the next day in the series, using LEAD inside of the DAYOFYEAR function to get the correct number. Lastly, we should select the basic columns so we can see the actual days.

Here's our <cte_body> query:

```
SELECT
  location, day,
  DAYOFYEAR(day) AS current,
  LEAD(day) OVER w1 AS day_next,
  DAYOFYEAR(LEAD(day) OVER w1) AS next
```

```
FROM precip
WHERE location='Raleigh'
WINDOW w1 AS (
  PARTITION BY location
  ORDER BY day
);
```

Here is what the first few rows of the result look like:

```
+----------+------------+---------+------------+------+
| location | day        | current | day_next   | next |
+----------+------------+---------+------------+------+
| Raleigh  | 1976-01-03 |       3 | 1976-01-07 |    7 |
| Raleigh  | 1976-01-07 |       7 | 1976-01-08 |    8 |
| Raleigh  | 1976-01-08 |       8 | 1976-01-11 |   11 |
| Raleigh  | 1976-01-11 |      11 | 1976-01-14 |   14 |
| Raleigh  | 1976-01-14 |      14 | 1976-01-16 |   16 |
| Raleigh  | 1976-01-16 |      16 | 1976-01-17 |   17 |
| Raleigh  | 1976-01-17 |      17 | 1976-01-26 |   26 |
| Raleigh  | 1976-01-26 |      26 | 1976-01-27 |   27 |
| Raleigh  | 1976-01-27 |      27 | 1976-02-01 |   32 |
| Raleigh  | 1976-02-01 |      32 | 1976-02-02 |   33 |
...
+----------+------------+---------+------------+------+
```

Moving on to the *<cte_query>* section, let's keep things somewhat simple by first selecting our basic columns and then doing some simple math on the current and next columns to define where the gap is. The start of a gap is whatever is current plus one, and the end of a gap is whatever is next minus one.

Gaps that are equal to 1 aren't all that interesting, because they're not gaps. A gap of 1 indicates a contiguous section of data—not what we're looking for here. So, one thing we need to do is ensure that gaps are larger than 1.

Here's our completed Gaps CTE:

```
WITH gaps AS (
  SELECT
    location, day,
    DAYOFYEAR(day) AS current,
    LEAD(day) OVER w1 AS day_next,
    DAYOFYEAR(LEAD(day) OVER w1) AS next
  FROM precip
  WINDOW w1 AS (
    PARTITION BY location
    ORDER BY day
  )
)
```

```
SELECT
  location,day,day_next,
  current + 1 AS gap_start,
  next - 1 AS gap_end
FROM gaps
WHERE
  next - current > 1
  AND
  location = 'Raleigh'
ORDER BY day;
```

The first few rows of output from this are:

```
+----------+------------+------------+-----------+---------+
| location | day        | day_next   | gap_start | gap_end |
+----------+------------+------------+-----------+---------+
| Raleigh  | 1976-01-03 | 1976-01-07 |         4 |       6 |
| Raleigh  | 1976-01-08 | 1976-01-11 |         9 |      10 |
| Raleigh  | 1976-01-11 | 1976-01-14 |        12 |      13 |
| Raleigh  | 1976-01-14 | 1976-01-16 |        15 |      15 |
| Raleigh  | 1976-01-17 | 1976-01-26 |        18 |      25 |
| Raleigh  | 1976-01-27 | 1976-02-01 |        28 |      31 |
| Raleigh  | 1976-02-02 | 1976-02-06 |        34 |      36 |
| Raleigh  | 1976-02-06 | 1976-02-14 |        38 |      44 |
| Raleigh  | 1976-02-14 | 1976-02-18 |        46 |      48 |
| Raleigh  | 1976-02-18 | 1976-02-22 |        50 |      52 |
...
+----------+------------+------------+-----------+---------+
```

We don't really need the gap_start and gap_end columns, since what we're really interested in is the size of the gap. In our case, since every row in our table means it rained that day, a gap represents the number of days without rain. So, we should modify our query to take out the start and end columns and instead calculate the size of the gap.

The size is equal to the following:

```
next - current - 1
```

The - 1 looks a little funny on the surface, but is needed because we're counting for the number of days between day and day_next, not between the next and current columns.

While we're tweaking things, we might as well modify our WHERE clause to only show periods of no precipitation that last longer than a week.

Here's our final query for showing the gaps:

```
WITH gaps AS (
  SELECT
    location, day,
    DAYOFYEAR(day) AS current,
    LEAD(day) OVER w1 AS day_next,
    DAYOFYEAR(LEAD(day) OVER w1) AS next
  FROM precip
  WINDOW w1 AS (
    PARTITION BY location
    ORDER BY day
  )
)
SELECT
  location,day,day_next,
  next - current - 1 AS size
FROM gaps
WHERE
  next - current - 1 >= 8
  AND
  location = 'Raleigh'
ORDER BY day;
```

The result looks like the following:

```
+----------+------------+------------+------+
| location | day        | day_next   | size |
+----------+------------+------------+------+
| Raleigh  | 1976-01-17 | 1976-01-26 |    8 |
| Raleigh  | 1976-02-22 | 1976-03-06 |   12 |
| Raleigh  | 1976-03-16 | 1976-03-25 |    8 |
| Raleigh  | 1976-04-01 | 1976-04-30 |   28 |
| Raleigh  | 1976-06-04 | 1976-06-16 |   11 |
| Raleigh  | 1976-07-07 | 1976-07-28 |   20 |
| Raleigh  | 1976-09-16 | 1976-09-26 |    9 |
| Raleigh  | 1976-10-31 | 1976-11-12 |   11 |
| Raleigh  | 1976-11-15 | 1976-11-26 |   10 |
+----------+------------+------------+------+
```

One thing is clear: April 1976 was a very dry month in Raleigh, and July was dry for almost as much time.

Islands

The opposite of looking for gaps in our data is to look for islands. In the case of our precip table, this means consecutive days of precipitation.

In some ways, looking for gaps is a much easier problem to solve, but thanks to CTEs and Window Functions, we have the tools we need to identify islands in our data.

The DENSE_RANK function has a property that is perfect for this task. Unlike the RANK function, which skips numbers if there are multiple matching values, DENSE_RANK never skips. For example, given the values 1,2,2,3,4, the results for RANK and DENSE_RANK would be:

```
+-------+------+--------+
| value | rank | d_rank |
+-------+------+--------+
|     1 |    1 |      1 |
|     2 |    2 |      2 |
|     2 |    2 |      2 |
|     3 |    4 |      3 |
|     4 |    5 |      4 |
+-------+------+--------+
```

So, if we have the numbers 2,3,4,8,9,12 and we DENSE_RANK them, we get the following:

```
+-------+--------+
| value | d_rank |
+-------+--------+
|     2 |      1 |
|     3 |      2 |
|     4 |      3 |
|     8 |      4 |
|     9 |      5 |
|    12 |      6 |
+-------+--------+
```

If we then subtract the DENSE_RANK from the value, a useful pattern emerges:

```
+-------+--------+-----+
| value | d_rank | v-d |
+-------+--------+-----+
|     2 |      1 |   1 |
|     3 |      2 |   1 |
|     4 |      3 |   1 |
|     8 |      4 |   4 |
|     9 |      5 |   4 |
|    12 |      6 |   6 |
+-------+--------+-----+
```

Any sequence of consecutive numbers will have the same value - dense_rank (or *v-d*) number. This number effectively becomes our island identifier.

You may think the RANK and ROW_NUMBER functions would also be useful for this purpose, but they both have issues if values in our table are allowed to repeat. Here's the same table from before, but this time including RANK and ROW_NUMBER columns, and how they would calculate it.

value	d_rank	v-d	rank	v-r	r_num	v-rn
2	1	1	1	1	1	1
3	2	1	2	1	2	1
4	3	1	3	1	3	1
8	4	4	4	4	4	4
8	4	4	4	4	5	3
9	5	4	6	3	6	3
12	6	6	7	5	7	5
13	7	6	8	5	8	5
13	7	6	8	5	9	4
14	8	6	10	4	10	4

With both value - rank (v-r) and value - row number (v-rn), islands get split when a value repeats.

Because we're dealing with dates and not simple integers, we'll use the DAYOFYEAR function to keep the math simple. Here's a query that limits itself to the Raleigh records and calls the day - DENSE_RANK result island:

```
SELECT
  location, day,
  DENSE_RANK() OVER w1 AS d_rank,
  DAYOFYEAR(day) - DENSE_RANK() OVER w1 AS island
FROM precip
WHERE location = 'Raleigh'
WINDOW w1 AS (
  PARTITION BY location
  ORDER BY day
)
ORDER BY day;
```

To keep the DENSE_RANK in proper order, we PARTITION BY location and ORDER BY day.

The results look like the following:

```
+----------+------------+--------+--------+
| location | day        | d_rank | island |
+----------+------------+--------+--------+
| Raleigh  | 1976-01-03 |      1 |      2 |
| Raleigh  | 1976-01-07 |      2 |      5 |
| Raleigh  | 1976-01-08 |      3 |      5 |
| Raleigh  | 1976-01-11 |      4 |      7 |
| Raleigh  | 1976-01-14 |      5 |      9 |
| Raleigh  | 1976-01-16 |      6 |     10 |
| Raleigh  | 1976-01-17 |      7 |     10 |
| Raleigh  | 1976-01-26 |      8 |     18 |
| Raleigh  | 1976-01-27 |      9 |     18 |
| Raleigh  | 1976-02-01 |     10 |     22 |
| Raleigh  | 1976-02-02 |     11 |     22 |
| Raleigh  | 1976-02-06 |     12 |     25 |
...
+----------+------------+--------+--------+
```

This query works perfectly as our *<cte_body>*. Moving on to our *<cte_query>* section, we can group our results by the island column and use the MIN and MAX functions to easily pull out where our islands start and stop. The only other part of our CTE to define is the *<cte_name>*, and islands seems reasonable. Here's the query:

```
WITH islands AS (
  SELECT
    location, day,
    DENSE_RANK() OVER w1 AS d_rank,
    DAYOFYEAR(day) - DENSE_RANK() OVER w1 AS island
  FROM precip
  WHERE location = 'Raleigh'
  WINDOW w1 AS (
    PARTITION BY location
    ORDER BY day
  )
  ORDER BY day
)
SELECT
  location,
  MIN(day) AS beginning,
  MAX(day) AS ending
FROM islands
GROUP BY island;
```

The partial result of this query is:

```
+----------+------------+------------+
| location | beginning  | ending     |
+----------+------------+------------+
| Raleigh  | 1976-01-03 | 1976-01-03 |
| Raleigh  | 1976-01-07 | 1976-01-08 |
| Raleigh  | 1976-01-11 | 1976-01-11 |
| Raleigh  | 1976-01-14 | 1976-01-14 |
| Raleigh  | 1976-01-16 | 1976-01-17 |
| Raleigh  | 1976-01-26 | 1976-01-27 |
| Raleigh  | 1976-02-01 | 1976-02-02 |
| Raleigh  | 1976-02-06 | 1976-02-06 |
| Raleigh  | 1976-02-14 | 1976-02-14 |
| Raleigh  | 1976-02-18 | 1976-02-18 |
...
+----------+------------+------------+
```

Things are starting to come together, but there is one final optimization we should make at this time. Looking at our results, there are a lot of islands that begin and end on the same day, meaning it didn't rain one day, then it rained the following day, but it didn't rain the day after that. We should filter out these single-day islands, and while we're at it we might as well filter out the two-day islands, leaving just three and above in our results.

Our first step toward doing this is to add a new column where we calculate the size of the island, like so:

```
MAX(DAYOFYEAR(day)) - MIN(DAYOFYEAR(day)) + 1 AS size
```

The only issue is the same one we ran into back in Chapter 5. We need to use a WHERE clause to limit output to just those islands greater than or equal to 3, but inside our CTE the WHERE clause can't see our new size column. So, as a final step, we wrap our CTE in a derived table wrapper. Here's the final query:

```
SELECT * FROM (
  WITH islands AS (
    SELECT
      location, day,
      DENSE_RANK() OVER w1 AS d_rank,
      DAYOFYEAR(day) - DENSE_RANK() OVER w1 AS island
    FROM precip
    WHERE location = 'Raleigh'
    WINDOW w1 AS (
      PARTITION BY location
      ORDER BY day
    )
    ORDER BY day
  )
  SELECT
```

```
    location,
    MIN(day) AS beginning,
    MAX(day) AS ending,
    MAX(DAYOFYEAR(day)) - MIN(DAYOFYEAR(day)) + 1 AS size
  FROM islands
  GROUP BY island
) AS islands_wrapper
WHERE
  size >= 3;
```

The output is as follows:

```
+----------+------------+------------+------+
| location | beginning  | ending     | size |
+----------+------------+------------+------+
| Raleigh  | 1976-03-30 | 1976-04-01 |    3 |
| Raleigh  | 1976-05-14 | 1976-05-18 |    5 |
| Raleigh  | 1976-06-02 | 1976-06-04 |    3 |
| Raleigh  | 1976-06-19 | 1976-06-22 |    4 |
| Raleigh  | 1976-11-26 | 1976-11-29 |    4 |
| Raleigh  | 1976-12-06 | 1976-12-08 |    3 |
+----------+------------+------------+------+
```

One thing is certain: that was certainly a soggy Black Friday weekend back in 1976. But at least Thanksgiving was precipitation-free.

Summary

In this chapter, we explored combining Window Functions and Common Table Expressions. We analyzed our precipitation data in various ways, averaging the days between rainfall, looking for gaps and islands of data, and even exploring how to turn a static column into a primary key column.

CTEs and Window Functions are the two most exciting things to be introduced to MariaDB and MySQL in the past several years. Now you know the basics and can start using them in your applications on your data.

Index

Get the eBook for only $5!

Why limit yourself?

With most of our titles available in both PDF and ePUB format, you can access your content wherever and however you wish—on your PC, phone, tablet, or reader.

Since you've purchased this print book, we are happy to offer you the eBook for just $5.

To learn more, go to http://www.apress.com/companion or contact support@apress.com.

Apress®

Printed in the United States
By Bookmasters